STORIES
IN MY
BONES

Hope you enjoy the Book

♡

Patricia

Mystical Connections
With The Ancient Stories
Of Rockabill

PATRICIA LANGTON

ISBN:

978-1-913590-98-7 (Paperback)

978-1-916529-00-7 (ebook)

Cover design by Lynda Mangoro.

The Unbound Press
www.theunboundpress.com

Hey unbound one!

Welcome to this magical book brought to you by The Unbound Press.

At The Unbound Press, we believe that when women write freely from the fullest expression of who they are, it can't help but activate a feeling of deep connection and transformation in others. When we come together, we become more and we're changing the world, one book at a time!

This book has been carefully crafted by both the author and publisher with the intention of inspiring you to move ever more deeply into who you truly are.

We hope that this book helps you to connect with your Unbound Self and that you feel called to pass it on to others who want to live a more fully expressed life.

With much love,

Nicola Humber

Founder of The Unbound Press
www.theunboundpress.com

In memory of my Mother Christine and in reverence to

our Great Cosmic Mother.

What people are saying about *Stones in My Bones*:

"Patricia's story, at its essence, is an exploration of feminine consciousness through the study of myth and mystical thinking."

Judith Shaw, Artist and Oracle Deck Creator

"Patricia's story will speak to many people on a soul-stirring level."

Nicola Humber, Author of 'Unbound Writing'

"The book explores the author's strong passion for myth, forces of nature and how it communicated to her a sense of great well-being."

Martin Keaveney Author

"Incredible. The parallels Patricia was able to find between her own life and these ancient myths was truly remarkable. It reminds us of the importance these cultural stories hold and the power and meaning they can give to our own lives."

Amantha Murphy, Author of 'The Way of The Seabhean'

www.celticsouljourneys

"It is a beautiful book of the Irish Dreamtime, a journey into the land and into the self."

Siofra O'Donovan B.A., M.A., H.Dip (PDE)
Author and Writing Coach

Contents

Part Four: Air

Part Five: Spirit

Introduction

"To find your soul connection with the land, you start where your feet are planted." [1]

Sharon Blackie

Have you ever had the experience of someone saying something to you or maybe reading something that resonates so deeply it sends your life into a tailspin?

The year was 2016 and I had just finished reading a book called *If Women Rose Rooted* by Sharon Blackie. Sharon is an English/ Irish writer of books on Celtic Mythology and connection with place. It is a journey to authenticity and belonging, as the subtitle reads. I realised after I read this book that I did not really have a meaningful connection with place or landscape.

I have lived in a town called Skerries in North County Dublin, Ireland for the past 40 years. It is a small seaside town with lots of natural beauty and a thriving community. Yet for me, I always felt there was something missing. I did not really know what it was. After reading the book, I began to think more about my connection to place and to the landscape around me.

While I was reading her book, Sharon was speaking at a St Brigid festival up in Faughart, County Louth, which is Brigid's birthplace. I went armed with my copy of her book to get it signed.

---

(1) See Notes section at rear.

She spoke so poetically about finding connection and authenticity in the landscape. When the session opened up to questions, a woman asked her, "How do we find this soul connection to place? Where do we begin?" She took the words right out of my mouth, as Meatloaf once sang. The woman had just asked the question that was on the tip of my lips. I sat there in anticipation, waiting to hear the answer.

"You start where your feet are planted," was Sharon's reply. Those seven words resonated so strongly with me. I could not stop thinking about them. I did have a connection with people, with organisations in my locality but not really with the landscape, and certainly not in the deep way Sharon had written and spoken about.

This beautiful seaside town has many wonderful natural features in the landscape that surrounded me, yet there was a void that I felt deeply. I came to live here in the early 1980s because my husband had a family holiday connection with the town in the 1960s. It was not 'my' place – I had no history here. So began the research of my local area to see if there were any ancient stories that I could connect with, or that would resonate with me at a soul level. "Where Do I begin?" I asked myself.

Stones Calling

I think my fascination with stone monuments was reignited when I visited Machu Picchu in 2004. I remember feeling mesmerised by the place. It had a mystical quality to it – very hard to put into words. Our guide told us how some of the stones were aligned with stars, and how it was an astronomical observatory. At one point, I felt the need to sit on one of the stones and meditate, which I did and was promptly told by one of the staff that it was not allowed and to please remove myself!

Something had been lit inside me. I think at some level in my being the stones were calling me in some way to venerate them and to bring their importance back. That is the only way I have of explaining it.

That year was also the beginning of what I refer to as my 'Stone Crone' years. I have visited so many stone monuments all over the world. I decided I wanted to see all the ancient sites that I could manage before I left this world. I was particularly interested in megalithic monuments and structures built by the Neolithic people.

All this foreign travel happened at the height of the Celtic Tiger years in Ireland. For about a decade, 1997 to 2007, the country experienced a huge economic boom. It was a combination of various factors like a massive increase in foreign investment, EU funding and very high levels of university educated young people. I remember at the time everyone going on numerous foreign holidays every year, buying new cars, bigger homes. I remember feeling very alienated from it all, as I thought that materialism, and consumerism had taken over. It felt like being on a merry-go-round that I could not step off.

While still swinging on this roundabout, I visited the Pyramids, Machu Picchu, Chichen Itza in Mexico, Petra in Jordan, the Ggantija temple in Malta, along with Stonehenge and Avebury in England. This interest in stones seemed to be happening in parallel with my spiritual journey, but I never really connected the two together.

I was also beginning to develop a deep interest in Female-based spirituality. I realised that a lot of these ancient sites were dedicated to women, and maybe that was the reason they seemed to be magnetically drawing me in.

This book is about what I uncovered because of this search. The more I researched Rockabill, the more questions I began to ask myself.

Why were these two seemingly insignificant rocks named specifically in our Mythology? Why was it a dog that they were named after? Why am I so obsessed with it all?

The Island of Rockabill lies just out to sea about 6 kilometres from Skerries in North Co. Dublin where I live. Rockabill (in Gaelige Dabhilla is pronounced Dawvilla – see rear for Pronunciation section) which means two lips in English. It is a group of two small islands made of quartz. They are called 'The Rock' and 'The Bill.'

The research has brought me from Rockabill Island to the Baltray Standing Stones near Drogheda, over to Newgrange and the Mythological story of the Irish Goddess Bóinn, to the powerful Formorian King Balor. It has brought me to our Neolithic ancestors who used the stone at Rockabill as part of the Brú na Bóinne Complex. It has brought me to the planets and the stars and a renewed connection to the Irish Tuatha Dé Danann. Above all these things, it has brought me a new understanding of my own life story and how the uncovering of local Mythological stories can bring you in touch with your own personal Mythology.

At one level, it is my personal story, but also, I hope, a universal one that You the Reader, can connect with. The Mythologist, Phil Cousineau, tells us that, "The personal and the universal dance in and out of our lives and dreams." [2]

The book contains a mixture of Archaeology, Astronomy, Spirituality, Mythology and Psychology woven together with my own personal journey. I have found it very difficult at times to separate these disciplines and have tried to make them fit together in a flowing way. I hope that there will be some part of you that is either moved by, or interested in, some aspect of the Rockabill story. I hope that the ancient stories and information will come more alive for you, as I try to integrate them with my own life story.

There have been several times along the way that I wanted to throw this project away. I had extensively researched all the 'facts' the stories, the references. It read like an academic thesis, and I absolutely hated it! Only this 'story' of Rockabill would not leave me. It was like a voice in my head telling me, "Write, write." I went up to the Cooley Mountains for a day retreat and sat with my laptop open to review all I had written, and I just burst into tears.

I was just about to press delete on the whole thing when a voice inside me said, your story is the story of Rockabill. Your life is reflected in the stories it contains not just your stories, but the stories of many people. I cried even more because this is not what I wanted to hear. So, I took a few deep breaths, calmed myself and thought about this idea of linking the stories of Rockabill in with my own life in some way. Maybe this would help me write the book I know I have in me but which was refusing to make itself known to me.

I reread what I had, and yes, some ideas about how I might do this started to emerge within me. The story of Broken Bóinn called to me about when I felt broken. The nature of the rock and how obsessed I had become with it was telling me about my stage in life of becoming a 'Cailleach' and about how disembodied I was. The story of Balor and the cow and calf were showing me how I became burnt out and how the eclipsed Feminine needs to be brought back into the world, and

17

ultimately how the story of Áed has restored the voice of the 'Sídhe' on Rockabill and their presence in my life.

Even though I knew this would be more of a spiritual and self-revelatory book, it seemed to be the only way I was going to be able to write it. To write in a way that makes the stories and all the aspects connected to it more accessible and relevant to me as the writer and for others too, namely you as the reader.

I also realised I was being called to write about the re-emergence of the Divine Feminine and how it was happening in my world and all over the planet. I sense it as a re-awakening of a connection to landscape and an uncovering of how our ancient ancestors viewed the Earth as a sacred place. There are people all over the planet who are listening to the voices of the ancestors and hearing the call of their souls. I am one of these people. For me, it feels like a veil being lifted from things and we are seeing how they really are. It is different for everyone – for me it was the discovery of two small rocks out in the sea near where I live.

Where is home to me? As a spiritual seeker I was always trying to find home in the outer reaches of the cosmos, the spirit world that is above, out there somewhere. Now, when think I of myself before I started this project, I would say I was deeply connected to Spirit in my mind, but my body was lost somewhere else. The writing of this book has helped me become more 'embodied' as a spiritual being and I hope it will do the same for you.

I have divided the main part of the book into five sections that follow the elements.

In the water element, I tell the ancient story of Bóinn and how her story helped me deal with the diagnosis in my forties of a chronic pain and fatigue condition called Fibromyalgia. *Her story was my story.*

18

In the Earth/Rock section I tell the amazing story of the white quartz of Rockabill. How our ancient ancestors viewed them as God stones and how this revelation transformed my relationship to my own body as I came into my Crone years. *Their story is my story.*

The fire section tells the story of the Sun God Balor who stole the cow (Moon) and the calf (Venus). This story puts me in touch with my anger about how women were burned and suffer with burnout. It also reignited and made me aware of my passions in a new way. *This story is also my story.*

The story of Áed is the theme of the section on Air. This very short and forgotten story gave me a route into the realm of the Tuatha Dé Danann and their connection with Rockabill. It also initiated my personal communication with these etheric beings.

Their story is my story too.

The last main section is titled Spirit. This is where I explore and share my own spiritual journey with you.

My hope for You the Reader is that these stories will resonate with you in some meaningful way as they did with me. I struggled with writing this book because I was fearful of what it might result in for me. My spirit was compelling me to write and tell the story and in the end my soul won out over the fear.

Reading This Book

This was supposed to be the section where I have some wise words about how you should read this book, which is what I had originally written and then deleted. I would not presume to tell anyone how to read a book – I would hate for anyone to tell me either. Everyone has their own way of reading.

Some of the writing may resonate with you; some may not and that is fine. I would love to know how you have come to have the book in your hand – that would be a much better idea. I know I have come across some books that I found randomly, some were suggestions, and some fell off bookshelves and shouted, "Buy me!!!" Some have had a huge impact on my life, some books contained wonderful ideas, others have come and gone that have meant very little. I hope this book will not be the latter for you.

I have included a Rockabill Reflection at the end of each section, and this might give you a chance to see how each chapter lands with you or may provoke a question to answer for yourself about the themes.

> *"To reflect on Myth is to reflect on oneself."* [3]

There are many themes running through the book. For me the main themes are healing, connection and freedom. Healing my relationship with my body. I developed a new connection with my body because of writing these stories. Healing my mind as I grow older and see myself in a new and exciting way as a Crone Woman in her power. Telling some of my life stories has also been healing and freeing for me. It has given me a connection to the place I live that I never had, and a connection to the Shining Beings who reside on Rockabill Island.

Ultimately my hope for you is that in the reading of this book you will find some form of deeper connection that will have a healing effect. Whether it be with the elements, the stones, the Sídhe (pronounced (p.) Shee) or maybe even yourself.

Chapter One: Mythology

"A country is defined by the stories it tells."

Dolores Whelan

A story that is carried through history and becomes part of the Mythology of the people, is one that contains insights and wisdom important to the development of the culture and psyche of the society.[1]

We all have our stories. The daily ones of whatever is going down in our life, and the more dramatic ones if an event occurs that we feel the need to tell people about. In Ireland we love telling stories, it is in the DNA for sure. More than anywhere else in Europe, Ireland has never lost the tradition of storytelling, including many stories, customs and traditions that were deeply enmeshed with Myth.(2)

Growing up in Ireland in the 60s, the two main Mythological stories I remember hearing about was *The Children of Lir* and *The Story of Cuchulainn*. One was about children being turned into swans by their stepmother and the other was about a great warrior. I don't remember connecting with them on any level or understanding their meaning when I was young. Now, had they been made into a Disney movie, it might have been different. The fairy stories of The Brothers Grimm and Hans Christian Anderson were more popular for me as a child. I had many books about these fairy stories and legends as I was an avid reader, but no Irish ones.

The stories of our Mythology are very much connected with

place in Ireland. I lived in the city of Dublin. My parents were opera singers and, in our family, music was what everyone seemed more interested in. In my experience, the ancient stories and Myths were kept more alive in rural parts of the country.

In the year 2004, during the booming Celtic Tiger years, our family bought a small holiday home on the Cooley Peninsula in County Louth. Although it is only one hour's drive from Skerries, it brings you into the heart of the Cooley Mountains. This area is steeped in the Mythology of the above mentioned Cuchulainn and the brave warrior Queen Maebh. It was also very close to the birthplace of St Brigid in Faughart. I began to want to learn more about the Mythological stories of the area as I now had a personal connection to it.

Paul Rebillot writes that a story integrates an idea of the *mind* with the feelings of the *heart* and the sensations of the *body*. Even if the intellectual message is not understood the teaching may be realised by the soul, beyond words.[3]

Before writing was invented, we told our stories orally and there was a need to remember them. The word Mythology in ancient Greek means 'Mythos' (story) and 'logos' (speech). So speaking our stories was the original meaning of the word. When we wanted to put images onto the planet, the first place we did this, was on stone. One of the first known images was carved into a stone in the Blombos Cave in South Africa 77,000 years ago. So we have had the human urge to tell our stories for a very, very long time.[4]

Myth as Meaning

Joseph Campbell is considered the father of Mythology. He talks about Mythology in a way that makes it very meaningful in our daily lives. *"When the story is in your mind, then you see its relevance to something happening in your own life."*[5] This has happened for me and is the reason I am writing this book.

It can also mean a narrative of such profound cultural and individual importance that it can help us establish the ultimate shape and meaning of our existence.[6]

So, the story of an ancient Goddess that was told several thousand years ago can be relevant for us in today's world. Myths help us to understand the world around us, as filled with its own purpose and meaning, rather than as a mere backdrop for human activity.

Myth as Spiritual Significance

Myths are stories with very large significance. Campbell tells us that they are clues to spiritual potentials of human life and they put you in touch with the experience of being alive.

Our Neolithic ancestors used stories and Mythology to give us clues about the spiritual potentialities of human life.[7] They are also about delivering timeless messages in timely ways. I hope that the Myths and Folklore that run through this book and how they unveiled my stories will give you permission to look at them in your own life.

Myth as Healing

One of the great healing functions of Myth is to show us that we are not alone with our feelings, fears, conflicts and aspirations.

There has long been a mythic link between storytelling and the healing arts – so much so that in some ancient societies, storytellers and healers were one and the same. Stories are valued in many indigenous cultures not only for their entertainment value but also as a means to

23

pass on cultural teachings -- including practices intended to prevent imbalance and illness (both physical and mental), and to help overcome ordeals of disease, calamity, or trauma.[8]

These Mythological stories certainly have given me a way of looking at my life which has been healing for me. Clarissa Pinkola Estés also believes that stories are medicine. She remembers having been taken with stories since she heard her very first one. "They have such power; they do not require that we do, be, act, anything – we need only listen."[9]

Mythology as Life

Mythology and science both extend the scope of human beings. Like science and technology, Mythology, as we shall see, is not about opting out of this world, but about enabling us to live more intensely within it.[10] Myth is not just about nature and certainly not just about the heavens, it is about life, and life is not reducible to any one approach.[11]

Myth as Locality

The landmarks mentioned in Mythic stories may be places that the story creators see every day in the distance, or return to every year in a pilgrimage, or even pass every day in their normal lives.[12] I pass by Rockabill every day in my normal life. There was a time when I would not even glance out to sea, walking around being so preoccupied in my own thoughts. These rocks held no significance for me in any way. Now I hold them in great reverence, as I would any other sacred site. And as I pass them, I stop, I acknowledge them and remember how important they are.

Myth as Universality

A Myth taps into a universal cultural narrative, the collective wisdom of man. There is a universality of Myth themes. Different cultures have similar Myths about great floods, virgin births, and the afterlife. The subject of Myths reflects the universal concerns of mankind throughout history, birth, death the afterlife, the origin of man and the world, good and evil and the nature of man himself. It seems all over the planet that Humans have the need to create Mythology.

As Paul Cousineau maintains, Myth is about delivering timeless messages in timely ways. It is now time to tell you the timeless story of Rockabill.

It is a story that is a bit fragmented with parts that have been lost in the mists of time. I think the story of Rockabill fulfils all the aspects of Myth that I have spoken about and hopefully you will be able to enter its stories with your mind, your heart and your body.

Rockabill Mythology

The Mythology of Ireland was only written down in the 12th century by Christian monks. Many of the major stories were included in these texts and some more minor ones were not. A lot of the writings were interlaced with Christian ideology, but most writers agree that the essence of the stories are there, regardless of the religious beliefs of the writers.

I am not going to outline all the Mythology here as many great writers have written about it in a more detailed and descriptive way than I would be able to do. I do want to give you a flavour of how I view the parts of Mythology that are important for this book.

The Tuatha Dé Danann and The Formorians

The Mythology that is written in the ancient manuscripts mostly contains stories about Battles. Some about place names. Many groups of people populated Ireland throughout history. The two main group of deities that are connected with Rockabill are the Tuatha Dé Danann and The Formorians. The battle of the good and bad are played out with these two groups.

The Formori were viewed as deities of the underworld, their name meaning 'under spirits'(13) From a psychological point of view, they could be viewed as the unconscious part of ourselves. They would have been viewed in opposition to the Tuatha Dé Danann.

The Tuatha Dé Danann (The people of the goddess Danu) came from the brighter otherworld. Some writers say they descended into Ireland in a mist. They were even known as 'The Shining Ones,' They are also known as The Sídhe or the Fairy Folk. The Otherworld can be viewed as the invisible world of spirit. The conflict of the Tuatha Dé Danann and the Formorians can be described in psychological terms as one of the light versus the shadow or dark.(14)

The Mythology talks about these deities as individual Gods and Goddesses. They can also be viewed as archetypes that inhabit specific qualities.

Bóinn

Bóinn is described as the Goddess of the River Boyne, which is named after her. She is one of the Goddesses of the Tuatha Dé Danann. Brú na Bóinne (Newgrange) is named after her. She is the wife of the God Neachtan and the mother of Oengus (who was conceived after she had an affair with The Dagda). She is sometimes named Bo Finn or Boand. Bo means Cow and Finn means white. Her name can also mean 'Illuminated Cow.' The second part of her name can also mean wisdom.(15)

She had a lap dog called Dabhilla and this fact plays a huge role in the story, for we are talking about this aspect of her connection with Dabhilla which is the Irish name for Rockabill. Lapdogs play a healing role for the Goddesses in our ancient Mythology.(16)

Cally

I introduce 'Cally' to you, who is my own fictional creation and I have used her to explain the ancient nature of the Rock on Rockabill. All the information about the Rock that Cally speaks about is referenced by me and I have researched it thoroughly. I just could not write about the Rock in a linear and academic way. I found that I had a lot of really great information about the stone on Rockabill. Every time I tried to write the story of the stones, it felt very academic, like I was making a list. I thought if I create a character to tell the story of the stones it might come more alive for me and You the Reader. I called her Cally because of the connection with The Cailleach and the Rock.

I have put all the references into an appendix at the back of the book in case you want to check out more about it, but I much prefer the idea of Cally telling you the story in a creative way.

Balor – Sun God

Balor and Rockabill

Another nickname for Rockabill is the Cow and the Calf. Why is this and where did the name come from? We turn again to Mythology for the answer and here we find another

Mythological story about the Formorian God Balor.

The Formorians were another set of people who inhabited Ireland thousands of years ago. They are usually portrayed as giants and monster-like creatures. They were considered the enemies of the Tuatha Dé Danann. If the Tuatha Dé Danann came from the sky, the Formorians are thought to have come from the sea. They were often portrayed as a race of god-like sea pirates. They had battles for control of lands and animals during the Neolithic era when they were in Ireland. One of the most famous of the Formorians was known as Balor of the Evil Eye. He was considered a Sun God. His name can be connected with an ancient word 'Bhel' meaning flash and he is known as a sun deity.

The story goes that Balor was in his father's fortress spying on the druids who were brewing a deadly brew in their cauldron. He pressed his face to a crack to spy when a vapour rose and entered his eye and filled it with evil. It was for this reason that Balor had to keep his eye covered.(17)

Balor – The Bubbling Cauldron

The Cauldron is one of the gifts that the Tuatha Dé Danann brought to Ireland – the Cauldron of Plenty. No matter how much it emptied, it was filled up again. To me the bubbling cauldron is a misty thing. It is a place where mysterious items are placed and mixed to become magical things. The misty mystery of the cauldron was part of the story of Balor.

Are we supposed to know what goes into the cauldron? How it alchemises what is put in and turns into something precious and beautiful? We try to force it; we try to get the formula without doing the work of the mixing. It is very much like the writing process. The putting together of all the subjects, titles, writings, images, need to be stirred together to create the right formula for the book and the way it is written.

Áed and The Tuatha Dé Danann

Áed is a member of the Tuatha Dé Danann and very little is known about him. All that the short piece of story tells is that he is of the Tuatha Dé Danann and he is a healer. His name means spark and he had a Sith (Sídhe mansion) on Rockabill.

The Tuatha Dé Danann were said to have come to Ireland from obscure clouds and mist. They are associated with the element Air and brought with them many gifts to the Country. They are in our DNA, as a people who are semi-divine beings and were here at the time of the Formorians. There were many battles between them and the Formorians who were said to have come from the sea or the underworld.

At a symbolic and psychological level, this is the forces of darkness and the forces of light. As I said previously, the Formorians represent the unconscious or dark side of us and the Tuatha Dé Danann represent the light part.(18)

Other Voices

There were times in the writing of this book when other voices seemed to be saying the things that mattered or that wanted to be said. I am not an advice giver, so the 'other voices' are more directive than my own voice.

I can try to name these voices and there were times when I was analysing them saying, "Who is that talking now?" for example. Then I began to realise that they may be various aspects of my own voice. They may be the Collective Feminine voice, or the individual Cailleach voice or the voices of The Tuatha Dé

Danann, but they are all coming through the portal of my brain and my consciousness. It might be interesting to talk about channelling here. When we think of channelling and what it is, it all sounds a bit scary. It always did for me anyway. Who or what is being channelled?

Some very famous books and individuals have written extensively channelled material. The Bible was channelled, *A Course in Miracles*, and most of the ageless wisdom books by Alice Bailey, are some of the most famous I know of. Here is where it gets tricky. Is it your own higher voice, is it another voice from the cosmos, is it a higher spiritual being that wants to talk through you? Sometimes I think a lot about this. Having experienced what this is like, I would say it is a very distinct experience of speaking the words that are not your own logical mind's words. In one sense it does not really matter who or what is speaking but the overall sense of what is being said and if it resonates. This is what I want You the Reader to decide. If a piece of the writing does not sit well and feels wrong, that is OK too. Be your own Judge. I have mentioned beings' names only because that is what came through into my consciousness, but I want you to be the judge of it all.

What I do know is this, the words that came through for me have great wisdom in them.

When you tune in or tap into the mystical, mysterious realms of life, something magical happens. There would have been a time that I would have so much fear about sharing what comes through for fear of being ridiculed. It may still happen to me following the publishing of the book but I feel the need to leave all the material in there that has come from the 'Other voices.'

PART ONE: WATER

"Water symbolises the whole of potentiality. It is the source of all things and of all existence."

Mircea Eliade

Chapter Two: Wells – Springing

This watery voyage begins at a well. The well of Segais (*p. Seggish*). This well is said to be the source of the two most prominent rivers in Ireland the River Boyne and the River Shannon. [1] We come into the world via a watery womb. Small steady trickling's that are the beginning of a birth. Springs form the source of wells. Dr Celeste Ray said, "The relationship between well water and spirituality could be as old as humanity itself, as they are watery, deep, represent beginnings, are meeting places, contain wisdom, and are healing and nurturing."[2]

In Irish Mythology the well is symbolic of the female womb, as they are passages into Mother Earth, they are often considered holy places. They appear in dreams as places of penetration into the unknown worlds of the unconscious. Places that are hidden and inaccessible in everyday life.

Wells are associated with the symbolic notion of the cleansing bath, drinking from the source of life, and quenching our thirst for higher knowledge.[3] Women have met at wells for thousands of years. They are seen as places that are the source of things. They are sacred places, places of the otherworld.

This thirst for higher knowledge is one of the reasons that prompted the Irish Goddess Bóinn to go to the well of Segais. In this story, the well appears to be the domain of her husband.

According to legend, there was a sacred well (Sídhe Neachtan) or Nechtan's Well, the Well of Segais. It contained the source of knowledge. All were forbidden to approach this well, with the exception of the God Neachtan, leader of the Tuatha Dé Danann and husband of Bóinn, and his cupbearers. Bóinn ignored the warnings, she was walking with her hound, Dabhilla, and strode up to the sacred well. She was curious and wanted some of this knowledge for herself. So she entered, walked and widdershins (anticlockwise) around the well, thus violating the sanctity of the area.[4]

Like Bóinn, I too have had a thirst for knowledge that is sometimes insatiable. When I want to do some research, I find myself going deeper and deeper, wanting to get to the source or what I call the 'essence' of something. It can be my undoing a lot of the time just like Bóinn. There seems to be a lot of beginnings, and don't talk to me about sources. It is interesting I am talking here about the source of the well, and I then try to look up what the source of that statement is. It is a result of being educated at a university and whatever you say in your writing must have a source. What about deeper knowing or 'gnosis'? Where is the source for this? Who can I attribute this to? It is as if this aspect of knowledge is unacknowledged. When Bóinn walked the well, she did so in an anticlockwise direction. Why was this? What led her to walk the opposite way of the male way or the conventional route? It was clear that she was breaching established customs and conventions.[5]

Was she Birthing something new? A new way of looking at knowledge perhaps?

Did she know from where the source of all life began? Was it all held in her?

Maybe it is about springing or bringing in a new source. Feminine knowledge is so very different to masculine knowledge. I am not talking here men and women but the masculine and feminine in every person regardless of gender identification. I think masculine forms of knowledge are considered more valuable in this world than feminine knowledge. There is a

34

disparity between them that I find difficult to explain. I have this battle going on in my brain about writing in this flowing way and it is fighting with the fact-based linear way. There may be times when I will switch from one way of writing to another, and I hope that you will be able to follow my way of writing. Like Bóinn, I will walk anticlockwise and find a new way of saying and explaining these stories and my interjections and re-interpretations of them, so they are like a new source, a new beginning. Sharon Blackie tells us that, *"In the old stories it is the women who make the world, so why can't we remake it?"*[6]

In the ageless wisdom (an esoteric philosophy that I am drawn to), the turn of the spiral in an anticlockwise direction occurs when there is an awakening, an awareness of a mission and this creates a reversal of the wheel. So, we are born or we incarnate in a clockwise direction and when we reach a saturation point, this awareness occurs and we then incarnate in an anticlockwise direction. When I heard this piece of information in a lecture, my stomach did a leap. I immediately thought of Bóinn and the well.

I know for me, this lifetime is about new beginnings and new ways of looking at the world. They are ancient and they are new. It is a clarion call to turn in the opposite direction and begin to see things from a new perspective.

Chapter Three: Wells – Bubbling

*"The Well waters began to bubble up from the bottom
up to the top of the well."*

Bóinn dared to do things a different way and everything started to bubble up to the top of the well. Another reference to bubbles is interesting here, as the Well of Segais is said to be surrounded by nine hazel trees and when the nuts fall down into the water, they form bubbles of mystic inspiration.[7]

I find it interesting that the courage Bóinn showed in going her own way led to a bubbling up of wisdom and inspiration. It reminds me of times in my own life when I went an unconventional route, and the courage I needed to make those moves, and the wisdom I gained from them.

I remember when I had a permanent part-time job in a good bank back in the 1990s. I had two small kids at the time, and I had what seemed to be a perfect job. I had time to work in the morning and then be home in time to collect the children from school. Working in a bank at the time was seen as prestigious. However, I found the work very boring and repetitive. Working in an office and what I call 'ticking and flicking' papers all day was driving me insane. At the time I was running a youth theatre in my local community and then I started to study for a degree in psychology and sociology to enable me to move jobs. The job in the bank was wearing me down and my soul was crying out for more creative and interesting work. So halfway through my degree with a diploma in my pocket, and experience in youth work, I applied for a job as a professional youth worker and got the job! Imagine moving from a permanent part-time job to a one-year contract as a part-time youth worker.

At the time, my best friend told me how courageous I was to do that. I did not think I was brave at all; I just did not want to be in a job that bored the pants off me. In some ways I jumped from a frying pan into a fire, as this work was very difficult. Looking back at this now, I was a woman in my thirties with a lot of energy and loved teenagers. I suppose it was courageous of me to move as I did and said, "Fuck it, I am not staying in a job that is destroying my soul. I want to be challenged, to be working with people and to be more creative."

It felt good at the time to be able to change careers and it did give me the wisdom to know that I can do things and make changes if I want to. I suppose I went against expectations of what others thought I should do and did what I wanted to do. I did not think of the money, the security or anything like that. I think at the time my husband thought it was a bad idea. He had been in the same job since leaving school, I remember pleading with him to trust me and that I really would be OK.

The bubbles of mystic inspiration are also a call to listen to your own wisdom. The bubbles from the well also move in an upwards direction. Other people's voices can be strong, and we can listen to them but ultimately, I think we always know what is best for ourselves.

Chapter Four: Wells - Gushing

"The waters gushed forth from the well to pursue Bóinn."

It turned out I never really got the chance to fulfil my role as a youth worker, as one week into the job, I had a bad car accident and it sent me and my life into a spin. I had a bad whiplash injury which pains me to this day. I remember, prior to this accident, I had a very strict view on work and considered myself a very diligent worker. I never went sick, only if I absolutely had too. I think I got this work ethic from my father. I remember when I returned to work after about two months of intense physiotherapy, my attitude to work had completely changed. It became less important to me, and I found myself after securing my first professional employment as a youth worker having no interest in it anymore.

At around the same time, I started to go to therapy because I did not know what to do – my life was so caught up in my role as a worker. This beautiful woman told me that when you are slammed forward physically (as in the car accident) you can also be slammed forward mentally and emotionally too. She was spot on, as I felt my life had utterly changed and I felt very lost.

Therapy and crying, gushing tears flowing, healing my wounds. I did a lot of crying back then. I have always thought of myself as over emotional, crying at a sad movie, when something good happens too. There is always a reason to cry. I notice too when we cry, we say sorry, we are apologetic. But letting tears flow is a very natural and good thing to do.

It is part of our watery nature and in the releasing of tears, we heal. If we hold onto the tears, it can go inwards and become unhealthy. I think there is more to it than that also. As emotional beings both men and women release it in very different ways. It may be part of our upbringing. Positive emotions are encouraged and acceptable, whereas negative emotions – anger and sadness – are less acceptable.

There are so many reasons to cry – sadness, happiness, wonder, gratitude. We hold it in so much. I have shed many tears of sadness, of joy, of realisation, of frustration. They have been teachers to me, sometimes the lessons are difficult to take, but my tears have let me process whatever is going on and my body is the better for it.

I found out recently that my paternal great grandmother, Margaret Vaughan from Kildare, was a 'Bean Chaointe' (*p. queenta*) – a keening or crying woman. I think I have her essence running through my bones too. My son jokes that every time there is a funeral, I am there sitting at the top of the church, crying, sympathising, empathising with the bereaved. The role of the Keener was to elicit the grief of the congregation to enable them to express their own grief. Sometimes the crying was gentle sobbing and sometimes it was a loud howling sound. The Bean Chaointe kept vigil also with the family as their loved one was laid out and 'looked after' them.

It is also possible that the Bean Chaointe took the role of psychopomp who's role was instrumental in ushering the soul of the deceased into the Otherworld. The concept of 'psychopomp' is a shamanic one and Angela Partridge[8] tells us there comparisons between the role of the Bean Chaointe and an ancient shaman. I found this so interesting as I have also felt this was something I was very drawn to. Just as there are birth midwives, there were also death midwives in the ancient traditions.

Chapter Five: Rivers - "Come on and cry me a river"

The waters of the well swelled up and were transformed into a raging river, a river that pursued Bóinn. In some versions, she was drowned; while in others, she managed to outrun the currents. In others, she was broken or dismembered and lost some of her limbs.

The movement from the well to the river in this story is not an easy one. The waters overwhelm Bóinn, she is pursued, maybe drowned, dismembered, or broken up. It is not a pleasant change from well to river. When I was reading this part of the story, the words like 'raging' and 'pursued' stood out most for me. It reminded me of my own inner thoughts and how they pursue me constantly. How at times of overwhelm, instead of raging and expressing, I turn in on myself and the rage turns into depression.

Overwhelmed and Feeling Drowned by Life

My Mother, Christine, died is 2006. I remember feeling very lost and abandoned when she died. It was a feeling of being orphaned. My father had died back in the 1980s, so it meant I was in fact parentless, an orphan. My sister got quite ill at this time too and instead of grieving my mother's loss, I had to look after my sister. It was also a time in Ireland of the Celtic Tiger and it was all new cars, second homes and big foreign holidays. I remember feeling completely alienated with all of this so called 'wealth' we suddenly had. It was like being on a merry-go-round, wanting to get off but not being able too. Everything was just so materialistic. It was like being pursued by this Tiger and I just wanted to run away from it. I remember thinking at the time, this is all going to come crashing down and, in a way, I wanted that to happen. I thought, "We cannot continue to stay afloat. We will all end up drowning." What was happening outside of me, in my environment was also happening inside of me and yes it all ended in yet another crash.

The Dismemberment – Being broken inside and out

'Dismemberment' narratives are common occurrences in ancient religions and Myths, and often represent profound metaphors for the disintegration of the status quo and the birth of a new sacred order.[1] The idea is that although Bóinn was killed or dismembered she then became the river and started a new life, sustaining the land. Although it appears the dismemberment is a destructive act, it is, in fact, also a creative act.[2]

I remember when I read this story about Bóinn, it felt so real and personal to me. I thought of how in my own life I have felt broken up, disintegrated.

In 2008, I was diagnosed with a pain and fatigue condition called Fibromyalgia. It is a not so well known and much misunderstood condition. I had to give up my well-paid job in the health services and much of the freedoms I took for granted, particularly around exercise and social life. It felt like my body was broken and no-one could fix it.

Fibromyalgia is an invisible condition, so it appears to everyone that you are OK, from the outside at least. When a flare up occurs, you are in pain from head to toe and have such overwhelming fatigue you can hardly speak. I remember I could not lift a cup of coffee; at one point I had such bad tingling running down my legs I thought I had Multiple Sclerosis. There are many other physical symptoms that happen in your body too. I won't list them all here, there is not enough room!

It has taken me about ten years to come to a place of acceptance and knowledge of how to manage my condition. It was like one thing was OK and then a wave would come knock me over again, I would have to stand up and try to bob in the water. There is a saying that time is a great healer and like Bóinn. who was transformed into the River Boyne and made herself anew, I have done the same, I had to.

In the process of creating the river, Bóinn's thighs were smashed, she lost a hand and an eye. Her physical body, which was then broken and created the River Boyne, a sacred river that would nourish and sustain the land. This is the idea that you have to lose part of yourself to gain another more transcendent part. That a death of one thing must occur before you can move on to a newer, more meaningful place in your life. I think this part of Bóinn's story is giving us a very valuable truth about living through a crisis and coming out the other side.

Every time I think of this story, I also think about the crane bird. Crane birds have been plaguing my mind for a few years now. They are an ancient sacred bird who were pets to our ancestors. When the crane birds sleep, they stand on one leg, and twist their bodies so it looks like they are dismembered. There are many Mythologies from around the World that have crane birds associated with them, from being messengers from the Otherworld, associated with wisdom. Bóinn became like a crane, to send us a message that even though we can feel broken, we can come out the other side and be a new, if different person, afterwards.

It reminds me of the shedding of the old, which can be painful and the emergence of the new. On a wider scale, I see this happening in the World with the various ages the planet goes through. From an astrological perspective we are leaving the Age of Pisces and bringing in the Age of Aquarius. Things in the World are being broken up, and a new way is emerging. I suppose this is happening all the time at some level in the world.

Old ways of doing things, like stripping the planet's fossil fuels, high levels of consumerism, old religions – all these are dying. But what is new and emerging in the world?

Losing My Voice

I remember doing a piece of training around loss and death, when I was training to become a spiritual healer. The exercise was about losing things that are precious to you and how you would feel about that on a scale of 1 to 10. Well, my body was OK, I did not score it that high (my disconnection from it was probably to blame for such a low score). It was giving me so much trouble – I would not really miss it and I gave it a 5 or 6. It went on to different aspects of ourselves and then we sat opposite each other in pairs and had to go into the actual feeling of what it would be like.

When it came to losing my voice or what it would mean to not have a voice anymore, I was devastated. I got so emotional, and it really struck me that I would not be able to sing or speak or make any sound. I have been singing my whole life and it was the only thing that I gave a 10 to, the thing I would miss most about losing.

I am speaking to you now with my writing voice. It is the same but different. When singing I am in tune, have a decent tone and can harmonise, it comes to me easily. With my writing voice I must work a bit harder on it, as it is a different kind of voice.

Chapter Six: Oceans

"The Feminine is a vast ocean of eternal being."

Marion Woodman

The story of Bóinn moves from well to river to ocean.

Bóinn was flung out to sea. She is said to have had her precious dog, Dabhilla, with her. Dabhilla was also flung out to sea, cut in two and turned to rock. The sea's current swept him away as far as the stony crags. Dabhilla is the Irish word for Rockabill, and the story is that the Rockabill Islands are the permanent rocks of Bóinn's hound Dabhilla. The water became the river that was known henceforth as the Boyne, and Bóinn thereafter became the presiding deity.[1]

When you read this story, initially it is the story of how the River Boyne and Rockabill came into being and how they got their names. Bóinn becomes the River Boyne and Dabhilla, her lap dog, now becomes Rockabill. The story comes from the *Dindshensas, Book of the Lore of Places in Ireland*.

However, if you dig a bit deeper, it is full of symbols and has a much deeper meaning. Sometimes when I read this story, it reminds me of the story of Adam and Eve in the Garden of Eden. It has similarities to a creation Myth, but also the power of a woman who will not follow the rules and pays the price for it. Another way of viewing the story can be a woman's sacrifice to nurture the land with water and thus it can be viewed as a death (of Bóinn) and a rebirth (The Boyne River) into something greater. This idea of the feminine deity being sacrificed to permanently nurture the land is also part of the Shannon Mythology.[2]

Dabhilla was the hound or lapdog of Bóinn. In ancient Irish Mythology, if a deity had a lapdog, they were considered to have a healing role.[3] Many Celtic Goddesses were depicted with lapdogs as companions. They were also associated with abundance and fruitfulness or fecundity.[4] The lapdog's role probably reflected the healing or regenerative aspect of the Goddess's function.

Flung into the Ocean

Of all the bodies of water that exist, I think the ocean is the one that scares me the most. I am not sure why this is. Is it the depth? The vastness? I also see the magnificence of the ocean. I have lived by the sea for the last forty years and it is something I kind of take for granted. I can go paddling anytime I want; I can walk by the shore and hear the waves coming in.

I have never been a swimmer. I am afraid when my toes do not touch the bottom. Some people fear heights, spiders. I have a fear of drowning in water. Not any type of water though, that is the thing, rivers are fine, I love lakes too. The ocean is a different thing. I cannot tread water, even though I have tried swimming lessons many times, it eludes me.

One of the reasons for this, I think, may be a past life issue. There is a theory that when you are on a spiritual path, your unresolved past life issues come back (or forward) for you to deal with them, heal them and then move on. I have what is called a living dream, or a vision of me being with my mother and being chased by a group of men and then we both are killed in water by them. It is not a dream at all, more of a nightmare.

46

I went in a kayak on my holidays recently and although my friends kept telling me it was as safe as houses, and I had a life jacket on me, every time the kayak swayed, I was terrified. I did not enjoy the experience at all. I did it but could not wait until it was over.

There is even a name for it 'thalassophobia' – fear of the ocean or deep bodies of water. I had watched in envy during the Covid years as different groups from all over the country went out swimming in the ocean. I did think about how wonderful it was that it brought back a real love of sea swimming for many people.

Our fears are very telling all the same. I have no fear of heights at all. I have jumped out of aeroplanes, can walk to the edge of a cliff and not have any fear. Up high OK, down below, no go!!

Poor Dabhilla was flung into the ocean and was split in two and was turned to stone. He is there out in the ocean for all time as part of one of the important stories of Irish Mythology. I will go out and visit Dabhilla soon. I need to go in a boat, with a life jacket and I will be terrified, but to see and touch the stones that mean so much to me, I will bite the bullet and just do it!

Face Your Fear

I feel the need to heal my fear of the ocean. I need to be able to go out into the water and immerse myself in it and not be afraid. If I could learn to tread the water, I think I might be able to conquer this fear. I am being called to do this more and more. In the light of the Full Moon, as I write in September 2022, I am doing a releasing ceremony by the sea. I will call on all the help I can to release my fear of the ocean and learn to love the depths, the vastness and be able to come up for air. I feel the ocean is calling me to embrace my hugeness, to replace the moisture in my body.

Like Bóinn who moved from conquering the well, to forming the river with her body and then to melding into the ocean, from Birth to Death to Rebirth. I too have moved from these water bodies and their messages to me, their amazing qualities, their stories.

The power of what tuning into nature can do for you – the transformation that can happen to you.

My mind is like an ocean. Thoughts that flow and wave in and out, then become repetitive and one after another do not stop like wave after wave coming in. There was a quote I found about the full moon and how it makes waves all the time. 'Making waves' is a term I have always associated with negativity. Don't make waves, say nothing, don't make a fuss. I still feel like that at times. There is so much I want to say but feel this strong internal message to not say anything. In writing this book, I have a fear of what people might think of what I have to say. I am now making waves by turning it on its head by saying, "I am making waves but in a positive way." If there were no waves, the sea would be a cesspool. There is a calm continuity about making waves, everything being the same, yet every wave is different.

I go to the ocean to do a ritual. I feel such a pull to do this, that it is all consuming. I ask two trusted friends to come with me. I can taste the salt of the water as it touches my mouth, I can feel the moistness of the water brushing against my legs, I feel fear but do not let it overwhelm me. The ocean will hold me. Bóinn will support me. I dip my whole body into the ocean. It is cold and warm at the same time. I release my fears into the ocean, I ask the ocean to take them away and transform them into waves that will heal. Heal me and others. I visualise them floating out to sea, over to the rocks, over to Dabhilla who will be there waiting to heal, to transform.

I have always believed in reincarnation. I think that déjà vu is a little glimpse into it that we all get from time to time. I read somewhere that reincarnation was a part of all the major religions at some point in time and then all references were removed from the Christian religion anyway. There are many scientific studies that show how through hypnotherapy, people go into previous lives and how healing can happen because of it. I have had this waking dream for a long time and wondered if it was a past life. It is quite traumatic, so I will tell it like a story.

Back in the olden days when wise women were hunted and killed, there was a teacher who taught girls about the world. She was unconventional and wanted the girls to live life with more freedom.

One day the Principal came to her and demonised her when it was discovered that her teachings were not in line with what the men wanted. They wanted to punish her, and they put her on trial in a court with a jury full of men.

She did not have a chance. She was condemned to death, and they killed her by stuffing a cloth down her throat and she died by being hung drawn and quartered. They did this because they believed she was evil and was poisoning the minds of the young girls.

It was me who was the teacher in this story. It was my living dream or nightmare and I used to have flashes of it come to me quite regularly. So, I decided to do a past life regression and yes the above story was the result. However, coming towards the end of the session I was asked by the therapist if I wanted to do the life review about what happened to me and what I learned from it. The message that I took from the experience was that speaking your spiritual truths would result in being killed and that I was holding on to this belief in this lifetime. So, I changed the belief and realised yes there may be some people who will judge me in a negative way but I wanted so much to speak my spiritual truth and this book is the result of that. It is a rebirth of sorts for me.

After the session the flashes and dreams left me. I still have a strong sense of them and wanted to include them in a longer story and maybe someday I will.

Rebirth

What am I rebirthing into? I really do not know. It is elusive, it is not clear and at one level it does not matter. I just know that there is a huge release of fear, that I am moving forward, maybe to make waves by redefining the stories that speak so deeply to me. Maybe something new is being born, then it dies and then there is a rebirth. It happens all the time in this cyclical world of ours. A wave is born. It lives, then it dies and another one comes along.

As Above, So Below

The Milky Way was regarded as a heavenly reflection of the sacred River Boyne, which is described as the Great Silver Yoke.[5] Another name given to the river was Roof of the Ocean. Many sacred rivers across the planet have been associated with The Milky Way. In Ireland the Boyne River is known as Bealach na Bo Finne (The Way of the White Cow).

What do I want to say about this river on the earth and the river of stars in the sky? It is that sense of a reflection of what is happening within, is also happening without. This is what sparked my idea to have a reflection at the end of each chapter. What needs to happen for me also needs to happen for the Earth.

All of these names are listed in our ancient Mythology as names for Bóinn the Sacred Goddess River. She is associated here with every other important river on the planet.

Segais

The Arm and Leg of Nuada's Wife

The Great Silver Yoke

White Marrow of Fedlimid

Storm Wave

River of the White Hazel

Banna

Roof of the Ocean

Lunnand

Torrand

Severn

Tiber

Jordan

Tigris

Euphrates

All these names are listed in our ancient Mythology as names for Bóinn the Sacred Goddess River. She is associated here with other important rivers on the planet. Like a river flowing out into the world and always coming back to the source.

Rockabill Reflection:

Personal: I feel that I need to heal my emotional life and that Bóinn can help me do this. By calling on her in times of emotional upset, when things seem to be going pear-shaped and when overwhelm begins to happen in my life. A message about letting flow happen. The idea of the well giving birth to the river and then flowing into the ocean can be a way of making sense of your emotional pain and moving it from a place of hurt to a place of healing. A way to do this might be to sit with a bowl of water from a sacred well, or a nearby river and ask Bóinn to come to you with whatever ails you and wash away with the water any brokenness or pain you feel.

Planetary: I also feel a call to heal our relationship to water in a bigger way. Our rivers and our seas and the pollution we are creating. We can call on the Goddess Bóinn to help to do this. A singing ritual at a well, a river or by the ocean – whatever calls to you – can be a way of sending positive intentions to the water. (I include a chant for Bóinn on my website irishstonecrone.ie).

PART TWO: ROCK

"In a crystal we have clear evidence of the existence of a formative life principle, and though we cannot understand the life of a crystal, it is nonetheless a living being."

Nikola Tesla

Chapter Seven: Cally's Story of Rockabill

When Bóinn became the River Boyne and flowed out into the ocean, her dog, Dabhilla, was flung across the ocean southwards from the strand at Baltray towards Dublin. And when he landed, was split in two and turned to stone, to become two rocks out in the sea now called Rockabill (The Rock and The Bill) or two lip rock, hence the name Da Bhilla (meaning two lip in the Irish Language).

To tell the story of Dabhilla, may I introduce you to Cally. She is a time traveller and will bring us on a trip into the essence of the rock that is Dabhilla.

My mother, 'The Cailleach' formed these stones almost four hundred million years ago. It was in a time before any creature or humans walked upon the planet. Her bedrock was shifting and changing all the time, but it stopped between what is now known as The Isle of Man and Ireland and these two rocks stayed out in the east coast of the Irish Sea just off the land, near what is now called Skerries in Dublin. It is interesting that the town of Skerries means rocks also. There they stayed for millions of years alone and untouched.

She made these rocks from white quartz. This rock contains so much magic, I don't know where to begin. This white vein quartz is a special quartz with very large crystals of white mica that enhances its glitter. The rocks also have a piezo- electric power that makes them light up in the dark when they strike together. This is a special gift my mother gave to the stones. They look like snow; they look like the Moon, and they have the Sun inside them.

Cally begins to move and shift and is getting ready to speak again.

I now want to take you forward many years in time to the Neolithic era where the humans of that time came to know of the power of the white quartz. They revered the land, the water, the Sun and the Earth. They wanted to make tombs from the stones and the rocks that lay in their vicinity and beyond. One of these tombs dedicated to The Cailleach's sister Bóinn was Brú na Bóinne or Newgrange, as it is now known – The Tomb of Bóinn – as it was built beside the river which she created. They called the white quartz 'na Clocha Geala' or 'na Clocha Uaisle.' This translates in English to Moon Stone or Sacred Stone. They were sometimes referred to as Godstones, but that was after the Goddess times, so really they are iridescent Goddess stones. Some even viewed these stones as a symbol of the soul itself.

Quartz comes from the depths of the Earth to catch the light that comes from above. First Nations people such as the Aborigines saw quartz as nothing more than frozen light, and light as the emanation of the deities above. The ancient shamans wore the polished white quartz around their necks. The hexagonal shapes that they contain is a model of our beautiful cosmos. They saw the crystals as a sacred place where transformations took place.

This amazing stone is also said to have beneficial effects on the entire hormone system of the human. It is therefore also the stone that helps older people who want to stay more active as they age. Because the milk quartz also has a good effect on the pineal gland, it can be placed under the pillow for sleeping. The increased melatonin excretion helps a person to get a good, deep sleep in which all repair operations happen. Mentally, the milk quartz has a purifying and harmonising effect. One recognises problems more clearly and can cleanse them, without harm to environment and family.

Cally now is wanting to come to the end of the story.

I know that it took the Neolithic people a huge amount of energy to move the crystal stones from Dabhilla and from Co. Wicklow to Newgrange and maybe many other places, where the people could harness the power of the stones. They revered these stones so much that they were prepared to go out to sea and travel long distances to get these stones where they could be used to bring them into a soul conscious state. The Cailleach is the Creatrix of all the stones, but I think she has a special place in her essence for the Sacred Snowy White Quartz.

(See Appendix for all the research information on the white vein quartz at Rockabill).

Chapter Eight: Rock Chick and Stone Crone

For the past twenty years, I have become obsessed with stones. Can what appear to be a lifeless inert object speak to you? I always feel that stones are trying to speak to me to give me messages. This might sound mad. Recently a friend of mine told me I was stone mad, and I think I am, mad about stones that is. If you believe in Animism, then maybe stones can and do speak. Animism is viewed as, "The attribution of a living soul to plants, inanimate objects, and natural phenomena."(1)

There is so much life contained in what we see as an inert piece of rock. Maybe they do contain some magical power, maybe they do contain the voice of the ancestors and even otherworldly beings. This has been my experience of them anyway. I have had some amazing experiences at stone circles and monuments all around the world and here in Ireland. During what became known as the Celtic Tiger years, when Ireland experienced a huge economic boom, I set out to visit most of the major stone monuments in the world.

To date, I have visited quite a lot of them – the Pyramids of Egypt, Machu Picchu in Peru, Chichen Itza in Mexico, Stonehenge and Avebury in England, Ggantija Temple in Malta, Petra in Jordan. Still on my list are Sedona in Arizona USA, the Carnac stones in France, Uluru in Australia and the Callanish Stones on the Isle of Lewis in Scotland. I had booked to go to see Callanish for my holidays last August (2022) but the ferry got cancelled. To say I was disappointed is such an understatement.

I took the summer of 2020 and 2021 during Covid to revisit all the sacred sites in Ireland also. Many I had visited before, but now I had a new perspective about the power of these special places. Places such as Newgrange, Tara, Slieve Gullion, Uisneach, Loughcrew, Cailleach Beara, Cruachan, Baltany and Grange stone circles. Ireland is so full of amazing ancient stone sites for such a small country. In each of them I always get a beautiful feeling of peace and serenity, a sense of the sacredness of the stones, a knowingness of something that is hard to describe.

Here are some of the experiences I have had at some of these amazing stone sites.

Machu Picchu in Peru

One of the most exotic trips was to Peru to see the wonderful Machu Picchu. It is one of the most amazing places to visit. I went in 2004 and I think this site was what started my fascination or obsession with stone monuments. It was a marvel to behold. We arrived at dawn and the mist surrounded the mountains. Then when the mist cleared, the amazing vista of the stone buildings came into view. I remember feeling awestruck by the sight before me. Although it was not the most ancient stone site, the altitude and amazing engineering feat of the Incas made it such an amazing place. There is also evidence that parts of the site are more ancient and may have been built in megalithic times.*
I remember feeling a palpable sense of something otherworldly there in the stones. All I wanted to do when I got there was meditate on the stones themselves. It is very difficult to capture this in words. It also turned out that there were only ever female graves found there.[2]

*See Freddy Silva's book 'The Divine Blueprint.'

Chichen Itza in Mexico

When we arrived in Mexico, it was to a beautiful hotel with a pool and all the facilities that you need for a most amazing holiday. Yet all I wanted to do was go to see Chichen Itza. I remember walking around the site, feeling very overwhelmed by the height of the stones, the way the sunlight turned into a serpent as it moved up the stones and the amazing sound resonance that emitted from them. Again, I was mesmerised by the whole experience, and I needed to lie down, which I did, right in front of the El Castillo Temple. Here is what I remember from that actual experience…

I lay with my back on the grass just in front of the main stone tower at Chichen Itza, I was very tired and just wanted to rest for a moment. Suddenly I felt a great surge of energy come up through my body from the ground. It was so potent that I could not move even though I tried. It was as if a magnetic force held me down. Then it just receded, and I felt such a sense of serenity that I did not want to move or get up. There was powerful energy there. I found out later that there was a well beneath the tomb where skeletons of young women were found. I also discovered that during the Mayan times that the descent line was maternal, with titles, privileges and goods handed down through the mother's side of the family. [3]

Although we were told that the temples were built by men, they had such a feminine quality about them, which I did not know at the time but felt the stones calling me to remember.

Avebury in England

I happened upon Avebury by chance while visiting the more famous site of Stonehenge in the UK The large stone circle has a village running through its centre which I thought was very strange. The very large menhir stones are such a wonderful sight to behold. All I wanted was to just be there at the stones, to sit on them, to meditate beside them. I was with my husband and there and then decided I wanted to come back here by myself to spend some more time as we were just passing through. He walked back to the car, and I said, "I'll just take a quick walk around the stones and meet you in ten minutes."

When I started walking around the stones, I began to have these visions and music chants came into my head and I began singing them. I had a vision of myself with a bowl in my hand dressed in a white flowing robe walking and singing in an anti-clockwise direction as if I had done this lots of times before. I was also walking with a large group of people who held fire sticks and we all walked and chanted together. I had a strong sense that I had been here before and knew the place and its ceremonies so well. There is one large stone that is a seat and I had to sit for a while, telling my husband that I was feeling tired. He went back to the car, and I stayed to take in the energy of the stones. I returned to Avebury on my own the following year, I felt such a strong connection with it.

Ggantija Temple Malta

We had planned a holiday to Malta in 2018 and I also felt the need to go to the Island of Gozo to visit the Ggantija Temples. These are Neolithic temples built around the same time as Newgrange. Upon arrival, I felt that huge usual sense of a strange silence and that 'special energy' is the only thing I can describe it as. As I walked around, it was as if I knew the purpose for each part of the temple. I felt a very strange familiarity with this temple. One section for washing a person, one for praying, one for being with people who were sick. I had that all too familiar feeling of the healing power that the stones contained and that the ancient people who built the temple used stones for different healing purposes.

The Pyramids of Egypt

When I was in Egypt, I could not go into or near the pyramids, as it was so hot. And although I was awestruck by the sight of them, I did not have any of the same experiences. I felt a very masculine energy at the Pyramids and did not get a chance to go inside them. At some level I thought that the stones themselves were calling me back to a time when they were used for veneration. A time when stone was considered a sacred substance. I also remember being awestruck when I visited the temple of the female Pharaoh, Hatshepsut, in Luxor. She was considered the most successful female Pharaoh in Egypt.

Chapter Nine: Stone Home

Most of the sites all over the world have alignments connected to them. Winter or Summer Solstice sunrise and sunset, Spring or Autumn Equinoxes. In Ireland, many are also aligned to the festivals on the wheel of the year. In the Irish or Celtic context, they are Samhaim, (now known as Halloween) Imbolg, (near St Brigid's Day) Bealtaine (May Day) and Lughnasadh (Harvest Festival).

Why are they so important to me?

Whether they are naturally occurring stones or man-made structures, they seem to embody the sacred. For me, they seem to possess a very distinct kind of energy that is inexplicable. Each time I have visited any of these sites I have had unbelievable experiences of a spiritual nature. It is like my bones want to connect with these stones. I can feel the spirits of the people who either made them or visited them when I am there.

Or is it something else going on?

Thinking back over the years that I have visited all these wonderful places; I probably should have kept a written account of the experiences that I have had at them all, as my memory is terrible. I have always felt that the stones were calling me in some way. That they had some important message that needed to be transmitted for some reason.

Some of the experiences were more powerful than others like there was a resonance in my being with these places. A way of trying to explain what I mean is to compare two visits. The Pyramids, for example, I felt had a very masculine energy about them. I could not go near the Pyramids as it was boiling hot, so did not get a chance to be close to them. I was mesmerised by the size, by the unbelievable visual spectacle of them. The Ggantija temple on the Island of Gozo was also an amazing experience. I could not wait to get inside. I felt a huge energetic pulsation there. I wandered around and just knew what each part of the temple was used for. I felt as if I was reliving a time of being in this temple, or maybe I just tuned into the frequency of the place, I do not really know why?

It is intriguing now, as I look back, that I want to do a Miss Marple on it all. Is there any kind of pattern, why after all the trips I did abroad, I then discover the fascinating story of the stone on my own doorstep?

At every site I bought a book about it. There is no doubt that some of the most amazing stone monuments in the World have a strong energy field around them, as people have come to these sites for Millenia to worship or give thanks or have rituals.

So maybe my visits to all these sites were leading me in some strange way to discovering the story of Rockabill.

Did our ancient ancestors know that certain types of stone are a way of connecting into some sort of planetary grid? When they began to feel the need to do this, they knew what to do. They knew the power of certain places and of certain stones.

There has been a lot of scientific research into the idea of a planetary grid that contains certain intersecting points that have much stronger energetic vibrations than others. They tell us that some ancient civilisations thrived around certain grid points.[4] When I looked at maps of these grids, most of them have been places that I have visited and have talked about in this section. With others I have not seen, I still have this huge desire to go and visit them.

So, at a level of me being conscious or maybe unconscious of this, in my small way, maybe I am trying to bring this back into the consciousness of people, the people who will read this book. Why me, why now – why not me, why not now?

Rockabill may not be the Pyramids or even the Skelligs. I sometimes call Rockabill "The Skerries' Skelligs." I believe they contain a potency, a sacred energy that is the same as all the other more well-known stone sites.

Chapter Ten: Cailleach Calling

I find it very difficult to be in my body. To be embodied. The ancient Cailleach, she who creates the stones, is calling me to be more in my body. I feel I always want to escape into my mind or into meditation or anywhere that is not my body. I do not feel my body as a sacred vessel.

I associated the body with stone. Solid. Heavy. Stone is calling me to be stable to be grounded. I think I want to escape from my body because of past trauma. I feel my body has not served me well. It has been the source of physical trauma and it is all stored in my body. I feel my body has been frozen in time. Still in shock, still holding on to the pain of the past. It is like my body has not recovered from the pain it experienced. The pain body is there and very present with me.

Any illnesses I have are of a physical nature. I seem to process stress through my body. My body always reacts in some way. I need to heal that, I need to move away from that. Let it go, out of my body down and into the earth. It is about letting go and not holding on. Letting go of youth, letting go of pain, letting go of having to feel useful whatever cause there is for the pain. Letting it be.

I feel a strong sense that the Cailleach speaks through stones. She is in the stones; she is the stones. Her voice is strong when I am around or near stones. When I get quiet and listen to her voice and what it is saying. To stop ignoring the calls that come in pain form.

While I was doing part of my Irish Shamanic training course, a chant dedicated to the Cailleach came to me. On the wheel of the Celtic year and in Ireland 'The Cailleach' (the ancient wise woman) rules and is the prominent Archetype of the Winter, the dark season of the year. She is the most ancient of Goddesses and is said to have created the land. There is one story connected with Loughcrew in County Meath where she runs across the land throwing the stones from her apron to create the landscape of stone mounds that scatter the land there. She is the ancient mother, the woman who has seen it all – the maiden, the mother the crone. The verse goes like this:

"Cailleach Cailleach, ancient one so wise,

 Help us, show us, how we make you rise."

I have sung this short chant a few times and never really looked at the fact that it is a question. How do we make the ancient wisdom of the Cailleach rise? It feels so vital, now more than ever.

As I write this, we are going through the Ukrainian war. We see daily the young men and women and families being killed. Toxic masculinity is at the centre of this need to dominate, to have power. The call of the Cailleach seems more pressing now than ever before. The whisperings of her ancient wisdom of respecting and holding the land sacred are becoming a shout, a roar in these times. How do we make you rise? I feel a sort of collective wise feminine voice speaking (maybe it is the voice of the Cailleach herself) and she is saying:

"Our ways are not the ways of violence and destruction.

Our ways are not the ways of violation and degradation.

We do not seek to exploit or dominate.

We want to show love and not hate.

The warrior in us is not the destructive kind but a slaying of the old ways in preparation for new ones. When there is a threat of the old leaving or becoming outdated, there is a holding on, a vice-like grip of wanting the old ways to stay. The wisdom of the ancient ones knows that this is useless. There is always change, there is always moving on, there are always cycles of eons and epochs. Now is a time of the setting sun, a time of loss, grieving and release. For we know that in the releasing of something old or dead, that something new will appear. That is the wisdom of the cycle. Just like in winter when the trees are bare, when the flowers are gone, when the bushes have no leaves. There is new growth around the corner."

So, this 'rise of the wise' for us as women now is in speaking our truths and listening to the voice of the wise mother, the wise woman, the Cailleach. It is in telling our stories. Telling the secrets of the stones. Letting the stones heal our bones, like I am trying to do.

Even though the Cailleach is not directly associated with Rockabill in our Mythology, I see it as her body. She is the one in the background guiding and directing everything. She is the one who is inspiring my writing and my interpretations of the ancient Myths connected with these stones.

In Scotland the Cailleach Bheurr is associated with the formation of various aspects of the physical landscape and is often said to reside in a cliff or a sea rock where she rules the waves of the sea.[5] I can certainly feel the influence of the Cailleach when I think of Rockabill. Her call is deep, her call is wide, her call is imminent and urgent. I am answering her call in the only way I can at this moment and that is to tell her story through my story.

Just as I was writing this, a video came up on my social media feed by a Scottish American poet Kris Hughes called *The Cailleach Rant*. She recited her poem and the line that struck me most was about "Dropping everything, society told us to carry." I begin to think about all those extra heavy stones I am carrying. The ones that compel me to help all the time. The ones that make me want to fit in with what others want instead of myself? The ones that I carry to please others by saying yes when I want to say no. The ones that say, 'Go and do,' when you want to stop and rest? The ones that say stick to your diet when I just feel like eating what I want? The ones that hold fear of being my true self.

These are not small pebbles whose weight I cannot feel. They are heavy, they are weighing me down, they are stopping me from being the strong and stable stone woman that I really am. She is sending me a strong message to let them go.

Short Reflection Suggestion: *What are the stones that are weighing you down? Is it time to let them go and let the Cailleach take your stones too?*

When you are in your winter phase, it is the Cailleach who will be there to help you rest, if you listen to her. In these times at winter, we are still busy, going, doing, pleasing, helping, nurturing, managing. We ignore her deep message of going inwards. Getting in touch with our inner Cailleach who is crying out for a rest.

She is also associated with wisdom. The wisdom of the elders, the wisdom of being all phases of a woman. The Maiden, the Mother, and now the Crone or the Cailleach. These are very specific phases we go through and there are many more in-between phases.

I find it interesting that when a woman reaches a certain age, maybe going into her Crone years, she can become invisible. Yet her element is associated with stone which is very visible.

I think the Crone, the Cailleach is rising and wanting to be seen again. It is time to listen to her wisdom. It is time to see the sacred in the stones. Her stones, her bones are **your** bones.

Chapter Eleven: Two Rocks, Two Stars

I look out at Rockabill, over to the Baltray stones and up to the sky to Sirius and Procyon and see them each reflecting each other. They are a pattern of three. Baltray is a marker for Rockabill and I see Rockabill is a marker for the two dog stars Sirius and Procyon. In the names, we see the associations also. In the Irish Language one of the names for Rockabill is 'Dá choin bic na sidhise' – Two little dogs of the Sídhe.[6] I think it was a message from our ancestors telling us about our origins.

I often sit and think about how our ancient ancestors worked out how to measure the exact time of the Winter Solstice and then were able to build standing stones to align with the sunrise at the exact time on one day in 365. It is amazing and an event that must have meant so much to them. Instead of getting caught up in the science of it, I just contemplate how much reverence they had for the earth and the sun and stars. It was obviously part of their religious or spiritual belief system, and the coming again of the sun or the rebirth of the sun was central to that belief system. The rocks are always there, the stars are always there (well as we see them anyway), yet the sun comes and goes each day.

It seems that Sirius still forms an important part of religious beliefs and spiritual practice. The Dog Star is thought to be the central focus of the teachings and symbolism of some secret societies that survive until this day.

So, from the beginning of civilisation to modern times, from remote tribes of Africa to the great capitals of the modern world, Sirius was, and still is, associated with divinity and regarded as a source of great knowledge and power. The star that shines brightest to us here on Earth certainly seems to hold a special symbolic importance to mankind.

Fifteen Names for Rockabill

Dabella

Dabhile

Dabhilla

Dabhillop

Carraig Dhá Bheola,

Cloch Dabhilla

Cnoc Dabill

Cnoc Dhabile

Abill Rocks

Blackabill

Rockabille

The Cow and the Calf

Dabillain

Sliab an Chotaig

Questions, Questions, Questions

I have found to date about fourteen different names for Rockabill which are listed above.

I was sure there was another meaning for the word Dabhilla. I emailed a professor of the Irish language, and he told me one of the possible meanings for the word is 'edge' or 'rim.' Yes, I thought, that makes sense to me because when you look out at Rockabill you think it is on the edge or the rim of the horizon, it seems that way at times.

It reminds me of the Mangan Manchan's lovely book about the Irish language *Thirty-Two Words for Field*, I could only find fifteen words for Dabhilla.

If you ask anyone locally about Rockabill, they will say something like, "O yes, that's where the lighthouse is," or they will always talk about the lighthouse or the bird sanctuary, which are two very important aspects of Rockabill. It is rare that anyone ever mentions the rocks themselves or all the ancient stories connected to them. I often wonder how they may have looked millions of years ago, standing out there in the sea without the lighthouse on top?

Judy Hall maintains that white vein quartz can be considered the "Brain cells of Mother Earth, as it seams its way across all continents and under the seas stitching the planet itself together."[7] Crystal Healers say that white quartz has power to absorb negative energy, that its composition allows this.

Do We Know About Rocks?

Our ancestors knew about rocks. The power of them. They knew that rocks contained life, contained the very stars that we are made of. If we are made of stars, we are then made of rocks too. They are part of us. The Mineral Kingdom. Quartz is sometimes considered the Goddess's in the mineral kingdom. I say that because of its association with the Moon, its lovely illuminating white, it contains muscovite which makes it glisten like stars do in the Sun.

White vein quartz is magnificent. It contains the source of stars. I searched a NASA site recently and they have found evidence of quartz in the star systems of other planets. Neolithic people viewed stones with great reverence. They saw them as a means of 'Bridging realms' and used them to induce meditative states.[8]

Stone was thought to be a living entity, what is known as animism. They hold the universe in their actual substance.

Why have two stones in the sea so transfixed me?

The gleaming white smooth rock that our ancestors so cherished is a mystery and yet they got in their boats. They only chiselled just enough to use to make their sacred openings and to guide them in the darkness.

What meaning did this precious stone have for them? We can only guess into the Neolithic mind at this time, a time when they saw the Creator's magic and looked to the skies with wonderment and awe. They moved these stones because they believed that they carried spirit and soul but also had a healing function. They wanted to have their precious white quartz to carry out their rituals to give added potency to them. They saw the stone as having come from the sky – The Milky Way. It was a way of making the stars shine on the land.

There is a long association between crystals and healing. This is not just a New Age phenomenon. Indigenous people used quartz for ceremonial and healing purpose. Crystals symbolise sacred space, wherein all essential transformations are thought to take place. Our Neolithic ancestors experienced the 'voice' of stones.(9) They used the power of the stones to transcend reality and visit the Otherworld. They heard the stones speak to them. I think I too have heard the call of the stones. At times they seem to be calling me to tell their story and hence I had to write this book. It would not leave me alone.

From Disconnection to Connection

As I said earlier, I have lived in Skerries, in view of Rockabill for the last forty years. I came to live here through my husband and did not have any real connection with the area. It was and is a lovely town to live in, but there have been many times through my life where I felt very disconnected from my sense of place and a disconnection with my own body. Local people will know that to really be a 'local' you have to live here for at least three generations. When I developed a life-changing chronic pain condition, Fibromyalgia, in 2008, it led me down a path of healing. It also led me to ask many questions about my relationship to where I live. People find great solace in nature, but as I started to discover my interest in ancient rocks, it led me to discover the amazing story of Rockabill. I have looked out at Rockabill and felt a bit at sea, a bit distanced. Rockabill and its story has given me a sense of place and of purpose too. Our connection to the land we live on can have a healing impact on our lives, like it did mine.

My disconnection with place has been happening alongside my disconnection with my feminine nature. My rediscovery of Rockabill as a scared place has given me a way to connect with my own sacredness.

I cannot seem to end this section of the book. I feel there is something else that needs to be written about, but I cannot quite put my finger on what that is. I have titled the book *Stones in my Bones*. I began to think about my bones. My skeleton. Off I went on a research mission. Looking for something that will make sense to me to finish this part of the chapter. I found a quote that jumped out of the screen at me. "Skeleton is considered the bridge between life and death. It is thought to symbolise leaving the old and departing towards rebirth."[10] The other piece that stayed with me and really confirmed why stones have felt so important to me – our bones are made of crystal, they are made of stone, of the very substance that is stone. Stones are our actual bones![11] One of the reasons stones can have a profound effect on humans is because the body is made up of cells and these can resonate with the same silicon dioxide make-up of crystals. Therefore, such materials can cause a vibratory effect based on the laws of physics through the transfer and flow of energy.[ibid]

Chapter Twelve: Baltray Stone Alignment

Up the coast about 12km from Rockabill Island at the Boyne Estuary, there are two large standing stones. It is thought that they date back to Neolithic times.

On the north side of Inbher Colpa, near Baltray in Co. Louth, you will find two imposing standing stones that have watched over the river for 5,000 years. This is the point where the Boyne River meets the Irish Sea.

In May 1999, two men from Drogheda, Michael Byrne and Richard Moore, made an interesting discovery. Michael placed his binoculars on the long axis of the larger standing stone and in the distance, they could see the Rockabill Islands. This confirmed the idea that Anthony Murphy had about a winter solstice alignment at Baltray. They deemed it possible that the stones had an astronomical significance. They returned at Winter Solstice sunrise, and they were delighted and surprised to see the suns orb rise over Rockabill Island.[12] I went to see the Baltray Stones with a local archaeologist, where he took all the measurements and officially confirmed these findings, that there was an alignment. When I read about this discovery, I had another Sharon Blackie moment. Were our ancestors pointing to Rockabill to tell another story, and if so, what story?

Marking the Winter Solstice was one of the most significant events for the Neolithic people. They saw it as a returning of the Sun, a rebirth of sorts. At Newgrange (Brú na Bóinne), the most amazing solstice event happens where on the Winter Solstice sunrise a shaft of sunlight pierces the back wall of the chamber and lights up the triple spiral design carved into the stone. It is known worldwide and apparently an amazing experience to behold. If you apply and are lucky enough to get one of the small number of lottery tickets to see the event at the exact time of the Solstice.

At the very same moment at the Baltray Stones, the sun comes up over Rockabill Islands. The Sun has another ancient story to tell.

Rockabill Reflection:

Personal: I find I constantly want to connect with the stone that is Rockabill. When I cannot do it physically (because it is out in the sea), I can do it in meditation. The power of the white quartz stone to heal, to bring in the essence of the stone into my mind, body and spirit. Our ancestors knew it and now we can know it too.

Planetary: Our planet is in trouble. If we view the skeleton as holding our body, then stone holds the body of the planet. Some of its most sacred and precious stones have been mined out of existence. Why do we adorn ourselves with precious stones? I think at some level, we realise the power they hold. Maybe it is time to view them as more precious than we do, so we can heal a bit more from the Earth itself, which houses them.

PART THREE: FIRE

If you want to shine like a sun, first burn like a sun.

Chapter Thirteen: The Story of Sun God Balor

A Winter Solstice sunrise was such an important event to our ancient ancestors. It was the time when the Sun returned. Symbolically, it can mean when the Father 'Sun' returns and penetrates the female Mother Earth. A new 'Sun' is born. This is the story of what happens at Newgrange.

The God connected with Newgrange is The Dagda, who had an affair with Bóinn as stated previously. Who is the Sun God connected to Rockabill that led to there being this returning of the Sun to Rockabill? He is the Sun God Balor, that we met in the first chapter. Here is the old legend of Balor and Rockabill.

The Cow and the Calf

There was a very famous cow called the Glas Gablin, belonging to the province of Ulster. No matter how large the vessel used to milk her, she could fill it immediately with rich creamy milk. She lived about the time that the Tuatha Dé Danann were in Ireland.

Balor of the Evil Eye, one of the Formorian Chiefs, was anxious to get this wonderful cow for himself. Now Balor had only one eye and that was in the middle of his forehead. When the giant was talking to anyone, he had to keep his eye covered. The eye was evil and had the power of turning to stone whatever was seen by it – animals, people and so on.

He and his servant went to the Mourne Mountains, where the Glas Gablin was grazing with her calf. He had the servant drive the cow and her calf to the province of Leinster, where he had his stronghold. He told the servant to keep the calf in front all the time so that the cow would not look back and know that she was leaving the province of Ulster.

The servant did as he was told, and everything went well until they crossed the River Boyne. The servant got careless and allowed the calf to walk behind the cow. Soon after, the cow missed the calf and she looked behind her to see where she had gone. Looking back, she saw the Mourne Mountains far away to the north, and knew that she was very far from her native Ulster, so she gave a terrible scream, the like of which was never heard before.

Balor heard the roar and he understood there was something wrong. When Balor turned to see what was wrong, he forgot to cover his eye and immediately the cow and calf were turned into stones. The two rocks stand today as Balor left them – the cow on the south side and the calf on the north side, The Rockabill Islands.[1]

A Lost Story

The Formorian Sun God Balor is mostly associated with Tory Island in Donegal. Like many of our ancient folklore tales they were spread around the whole country. There are remnants of the Formorian Mythology in Farney, County Monaghan and these connect Balor and his famous Glasgavlen (Glas Gablin), not just with Tory Island in Donegal but from South Monaghan to Rockabill islands off the coast of Dublin.[2]

Henry Morris was told that when Ulstermen came to reap the harvest, they went to see 'The Cow and the Calf,' the two islands off the coast of Co Dublin, Rockabill. He also states that there are different versions of this story in Cork, Kerry, Sligo Mayo as well as Donegal and that it is, "Clear that the legend was once common to the whole of Ireland." He maintains that if all the remnants still surviving were picked up and pieced together, we might have a valuable piece of Old Irish Mythology.

Another example of this is *The Story of the Glasgavlen* also referred to as *The Story of the Fairy Cow* in parts of Co Clare. In this version of the story, the cow supplied milk to the poor people of the parish. She was a white cow, and you could milk her a million times and she'd still supply milk.[3] Are we seeing here another connection with Bóinn and The Milky Way?

The story about Balor was recorded in the Irish Heritage Duchas archives by Mary Halligan, who died in Skerries in 1906. It was also told practically word for word by another unnamed student in Balbriggan Co Dublin, a larger town 6km north of Skerries. The date for this telling is not given but these stories were collected in the 1930s and were told by young primary school students. These show at that time there were people in the locality of North County Dublin who were aware of this ancient legend connected to Rockabill.

Meaning

What does the story mean? As in many Mythological stories, there may be several meanings. Anthony Murphy of Mythical Ireland maintains that it may have an astronomical meaning and the story is capturing a rare astronomical event at Winter Solstice where the Crescent Moon and Venus meet. In his book *Island of The Setting Sun*, he links the movements of the Sun represented by Balor. The Moon as it moves, is represented by the Cow and Venus represented by the Calf. Below I will try to relate a basic version of what happens, but I urge anyone who has an interest to look it up in more detail in his wonderful book.

It basically tells us in this journey the Moon is always behind

Venus, then at one point in the cycle, Venus lags behind the Moon, and this part is where the cow yells out and Balor forgets to cover his eye and the cow and calf are turned into stone. The Sun petrifies the Moon and Venus.[4] The Moon and Venus disappear as the Morning Sun appears.

Chapter Fourteen: Seeing Red

When I read this story and this possible meaning behind it, instead of feeling the warmth of the Sun, I felt very hot and very bothered. Cows have always been associated with Goddesses. The oldest name for Bóinn taken from Bou-vinda means "The white lady with bovine attributes."[5] There is also a bovine association with the Morning Star, Venus, which was dedicated to, "That Great Mother symbolised by the heifer or the Golden Calf."[6] Here are two planets, so to speak, that represent the Mother, the Feminine and they are being 'burned' or turned to stone by a male Sun God, Balor. To say I had a visceral reaction was an understatement.

My Mother, Christine Murphy, had a saying if she got really angry about something, "It would make your blood boil"! Well, my blood started to boil when I read this. On the surface the story is about how Rockabill came into being, and it may well have been a way of interpreting an astronomical event in the skies by our foremothers and fathers, but for me it has a deeper and more powerful meaning. The burning and dismissal of the Feminine by the dominance of the masculine. Even the beginning of the story when Balor 'steals' the Glas Gablin. It may be that the sun blinds the moon and Venus but what it represents to me is so much more than that. To say it sent me into a tizzy is quite the understatement.

Anger

I wrote a poem about five years ago called *Otherworlds*. I want to share it with you.

Otherworlds

I have travelled a road of unseen things,

a journey more deliberate than casual,

whisperings from birth that diverts

towards depth and uncertainty.

I crash and bump,

while another me looks on and knows

where it all leads.

The sensitivity of living burns

a fire in my soul, quenched

by the water of life.

Winds of change remain.

On this earth and in

Otherworlds, the next chain begins…

One of the lines from this poem reads, "The sensitivity of living burns a fire in my soul." Sometimes when I write poetry, the words just flow out of me from a place I cannot explain, and they always seem to have a mystical quality to them. I am not a great poet (judging Trish), but they seem to write me and not me them. I used to wonder what people meant when they said that. But now this is what happens to me. A kind of mist comes over me, I go into a slight (only slight) reverie and the words just fall out onto the page.

"The sensitivity of life burns" – this is the hot, sore burning part.

It is Fire as Mire. I think of women put on trial as witches at the stakes, a way in which women were burned in the past. I detailed the past life I had teaching the young girls and I had my life snuffed out because of my beliefs.

I was put in my place, it was death.

I re-lived this life under hypnosis, and it was a horribly unpleasant experience. I think many women carry this burning wound inside them, I know I do. In Lucy Pearce's book Burning Woman, she talks about the burning times of old but says that even now women are burned for speaking their own truth. They may be healers, or witches. In societies today, where belief in magic is still present, women are killed. In Tanzania and Ghana as recently as 2012, 500 women a year were killed, and 2,100 women were burned as witches in India.(7) She also talks about how women turn their anger inwards into sadness and depression, and how boys and men can outwardly express anger, it is even encouraged. Now as I am writing this, a young girl in Iran was killed for not wearing the right covering on her head.

They were all put in their place.

When I was ten or eleven years old my Mother was in hospital for a few days having a hysterectomy. My Father had made us all a stew for the third evening in a row. It was the only dinner he could make, and he asked me to wash and dry the dishes. I have three older brothers and they were all out playing. I asked my father why the boys could not help me do the dishes and he said, "Patricia, you will have to do the dishes when you get older anyway, so you need the practice."

I was put in my place.

Well, I remember feeling like I wanted to lash out and hit him.

I felt so angry, it felt so deeply unfair, but I could not express this to him. I had to hide my anger, I probably went quiet or just finished the dishes and went to my room for a cry. It was a small incident, and in my head, it reiterated that boys could do what they wanted and girls could not. I loved my Father dearly and he worked very hard to provide for our family of eight children, but he was a man of his era and that was the way things were back in the 1970s.

I could talk here about a million things that make me angry then and now – how I still bury it – because I still feel a sense of helplessness and probably fear about expressing it. I was reading another book recently and came across the phrase 'Sacred Rage.' So instead of what is considered an angry bitch type rage, this is an explosion of wildfire that is both appropriate and timely. This sacred rage of the Fierce Feminine burns through all the lies, illusions, and distortions.[8]

In the last chapter, I talked about the wisdom of Cailleach rising, now I would love to see the sacred rage of the Feminine rising too, I think it is time!

As I write this piece, it is late afternoon and I feel the need to leave the writing and go for a walk, as there is another anger rising in me. I need to feel the anger. I feel it is as an anger that is the same age as me yet much older than me. It is an ancient but new deep anger for all the women that have ever felt it and for whatever reason. I shed a lot of angry tears for them. All I see around me is red. Berries on trees, leaves that were green are now red too.

I want the red to turn to orange – amber – a nicer, warmer colour. Still the red is calling me not to bury the anger but expresses it. Not to turn it from red to the blackness of depression – to express it not to repress it. I do not want to express my anger in a destructive way, it hurts others, and it hurts me. I need to burn with the fire of expression and passion, not with flames that eat me up and leave only ashes. I turn my rage onto the page.

Chapter Fifteen: From Fire to Passion

There is a phrase that is attributed to Marianne Williamson about fearing our light, playing it small, who am I to... etc. I have always read that quote and it hit at a surface level for the most part. I have never really thought about it in any depth. What is this fear about? Are we that afraid to be seen to be heard to speak our truth? I think it goes way back to the Mythology of Eve. The shame of making a decision, hiding our beautiful nakedness, and only being part of a human being i.e. the rib. Having predetermined roles in society, at home, in the workplace, the list really is endless. 'Letting your light shine' – what does that mean? It may well be aimed at men too, conforming to norms set by Patriarchy. When do we really look at a person and see them in their totality and watch what lights them up, what gets their juices flowing and what they are naturally great at?

Thinking these thoughts reminds me of when I started in second level school at the age of twelve. We did a year-long project called IDE, Inter Disciplinary Enquiry. It sounded very interesting, and I think it was to try to teach in ways that were a bit different. I remember I did a project on making some sort of cardboard replica of the Aswan Dam or something stupid like that. I loved singing and dancing and when I saw that some of the other groups were doing that, I was distraught. The project I was allocated dulled my light, whereas if I was on stage singing and dancing, my light would have shone.

Looking back at my twelve-year-old self now, I would not have been allowed to say anything or even articulate what I was feeling.

Hindsight is a great thing and for my light to glow I should have been in a performing arts school. It was the 70s in Dublin, Ireland so that was the kind of thing that you did as a hobby or after school. Artistic expression did not hold the same value as other expressions like sport or the three Rs reading, writing, arithmetic. It is a different time we live in now; or is it? Is artistic expression given equal importance to other pursuits?

Stealing the light can mean taking it away from us. This is what came to me when I read the story of Balor and the Cow with abundant milk (Glas Gablin). When we are in a natural setting doing what we want to do, playing to our strengths, we shine, we excel, and we thrive. If we are limited, put into a box or made to 'fit in' to a system that limits us, we have to strive, and we are a duller version of ourselves.

If you are lucky enough that your talents and strengths are Maths, History and Physics, go you. If you have artistic leanings, the standard educational system will not fully cater to your innate abilities, and they then go undervalued. I think it is time to recognise that each child has a way of expression that is unique to them, and I think the time has come that we let our lights shine, our hearts soar, our dancing moves enchant, and our beautiful voices be heard.

Being robbed of your essence, your essential nature. Balor is not just representative of Patriarchy but the system that it has created, that steals the essence of us all. Balor is the external light and the Cow and Calf, our internal light that is hidden and dimmed.

Too Sensitive

Then I look at the word 'sensitive.' I have been told that I am 'too' sensitive. There are many words for people who are too sensitive – empaths, emotionally sensitive people or EMPs. All my physical conditions could be viewed as having a sensitive body – IBS (irritable bowel syndrome), Underactive Thyroid (sensitive Thyroid), Fibromyalgia (sensitive to fucking everything). I believe that I am OK and that it's the World that is not. My system is unable to function to its full capacity in a world where we are all burning in so many ways. I left my job due to burn out. I was an arid wasteland of a person, so how can a body take it all? In the movie The Green Mile, the guy who is imprisoned for the murder of two young girls has a healing gift that sustains life and yet he is tortured by the sensitivity of feeling everything. I often wondered why I have watched this film dozens of times and it is a vague familiarity and 'empathy' with this man.

Burnout

There are so many women and men I know who have driven themselves so hard they have suffered burn out. It is usually connected with work or a job they do. They are so driven by doing and going, that they literally burn out or stop. Like a car with an overheated engine, the result of which you just stop and cannot get started again from utter exhaustion or you explode with rising blood pressure and have a heart attack.

My own burnout came around the year of the millennium. I was working in a full-time job, studying for a masters degree, running a local youth theatre on a voluntary basis, and trying to look after my two sons, plus run a home. No wonder I crashed and burned. I remember having the constant feeling of completely overdoing it and having severe headaches every evening. Going from work, then home, to college then rehearsals, was so exhausting. I was in overdoing mode so much I could not sleep at night, as there were too many spinning plates to keep my overactive mind even busier!

Something had to give. I had also gained a huge amount of weight because I was just shovelling the food into my mouth, as I had no time to plan or cook any healthy meals. It was also mindless eating mainly fast food, to cope with the stress. I eventually had to give up my job due to being totally burned out.

Balance – Re-balance

When you make a discovery and uncover something in your external world, you also make a discovery about your internal world. My internal world can be filled with drama and emotion. When I look back at my life I think of the times when I have fed my innateness for harnessing drama and conflict.

I find conflict very difficult and yet I always want to resolve an issue that I find conflictual. I find I can get on an emotional rollercoaster and the ride can last for a few moments or a few hours and I am left reeling in a tizzy afterwards. It is exhausting and a part of myself I dislike. I want to be a more even-tempered person. I want to be able to not react so intensely to a situation that does not warrant it.

It can be labelled as having an artistic temperament, over emotionality, over sensitivity, over, over, over the top. It usually grips me when I want to say something but cannot, when I want to express a frustration but can't do it. The emotion builds and builds and then whoosh!! It spills over into a crying binge or a tantrum or a withdrawal into myself.

Thoughts turn to feeling very sorry for myself, negative self-talk, victim mode and at its worst can lead to a feeling of depression. I am so aware of these traits and states within myself, that it is painful to even think about. When you are so far away from letting things go, going with the flow, accepting myself the way I am. Shining a light into the areas of my personality that I really want to remain hidden feels really fearful.

I am reading a book at the moment, *When Women were Dragons* by Kelly Barnhill. In this story when women become angry, they transform into dragons and they burn everything that has angered them. The book is set in the fifties, going into the sixties and it is usually men that get burned because of their subjugation of women.[9]

I have felt that heat alright, the heat of anger that makes your skin warm, then hot, then burning and fiery, it is not pleasant. You drink water to quench the anger, sometimes wine if you want to really bury it. I tend to say things with a couple of glasses of wine that I wanted to say while drinking the water but could not say.

Whether drowning in water, being burned by fire, or whooshed along by a gale of emotion, I need to plant my feet firmly on the earth or put my back up against the stones to feel grounded again. To feel whole, to feel the balance of things. The fire in my head gets too much for me, I want to get out of my head and into my body. I feel the need to do this much more often now than before. It cools me, it feeds me, it releases me from the prison of my negative thoughts. I think it takes them all in, sorts them out and they come back eased, calmed and more stable than before.

Other Side of Sensitivity

On the other side of this, the World is such a beautiful place. With many beautiful beings from all the kingdoms in support of each other. Life is beautiful too. The sensitivity of the World can let me see this part also. What beauty there is in creation, in the natural world, the waters, the earth, the air and yes even the sun that sustains us. The inspiration of creativity which has given us many wonderful things to help life along. This is the part that burns a fire in my soul. The passion that life has for living. The ability of the World and everyone in it to be amazing, the hope the World will become more sensitive to passion and pain.

Chapter Sixteen: Sun Goddess

In Irish Mythology the opposite of the Sun God Balor is the Solar Goddess and Fairy Queen Áine. Áine is the Goddess of the Summer Solstice in Ireland. She is known as a fairy queen of the Tuatha Dé Danann, and her name means 'brightness' or 'illuminated splendour.'[10] She is connected to Knockainey (Áine's Hill) and Lough Gur, Co Limerick. Her retreat is said to be at the Grange Stone Circle which is the biggest stone circle in Ireland with 113 stones. The entrance is aligned with the Summer Solstice sunrise. Áine's light can encourage us to shine our light into the World and that is what inspires me to write.

She represents a fiery passion, the love element. The magical Sun that is the source of all life. The Sun is usually considered to be male and the Moon female. I love the fact that there is a fiery Fairy Queen Goddess Áine in our Mythology. She tells the story of the life-giving aspects of the Sun, as opposed to the destructive side represented by Balor. She is associated with fertility and a great Goddess to help us live our passions. I have also written a chant to Áine:

"Áine our radiant Queen

Guide us to be heard and be seen.

Light our path with your magical Sun

With love in our hearts for everyone."

Connection to My Life

In my own life, I have always felt that I was living in a way that was not the real me. I always thought that I had to 'fit in' to a life that was not in line with my true nature. I did not have words for it at the time and always thought I am in the wrong job, or I need to see this particular event (whatever it happened to be) in a different light. Now I believe I was trying to fit my feminine life into a masculine way of living. We can talk about Patriarchy, politics, and all of that but, really, I think it was a completely unbalanced way of living.

Anything that is repressed or subjugated will come out eventually and sometimes in a destructive way. Balor can be seen as the destructive and dark forces of the Masculine and the Cow and Calf as the creative forces of the Feminine.[11] Maybe it is only when we acknowledge the darkness in ourselves and integrate them, that we can become balanced. This is the message that the story holds for me anyway. As a woman, I can find it very difficult to express anger or to feel in conflict with someone. When my anger is held inside and supressed or when I feel the need to speak up and cannot, it turns into illness in my body.

I have had some illnesses that have rendered me immobile, so my body at times feels like stone. So instead of the Sun being a destructive force, that it would in effect 'shine a light' on elements that need to become balanced.

I also think the Balor story can be used to look at how our planet has been devastated by climate change. All the elements have a role in this, but in this story, it is the Sun and the harm it can do by overheating the planet. Symbolically, the Sun burned up The Moon and Venus and turned them to stone. This ancient story speaks to me today of how I, as a person, needed to change, and perhaps it is a message about how we need to change the planet also.

Burning and Warming

The idea of burning also has two sides. Burning can scorch, kill, and maim. Burning can also be passion, heat us and again symbolically burn away negativity. It can have two very different sides like The Áine side and the Balor side. This story or legend has so many different meanings for me. In some literature, a cyclops with one eye was also seen as a God with two faces a bit like Janus the Latin God.[12] Balor is said to have had one eye in the middle of his face, he was a cyclops-type figure.

Sunny Face, Dark Face

If the face you want the World to see is a social face the 'nice or good' side of you, what is the other face? The one turned away from everyone, the one that no-one sees, not even those closest to you. We keep away part of ourselves all the time for various reasons. This idea of being two-faced, I think applies to all of us. Being a Gemini, this idea sits well for me. Gemini is the twin and I always associate it with having a very sociable side, and then having a very introverted and quiet side, again this could easily apply to all of us to some extent.

Chapter Seventeen: As Above, So Below

The name for Venus in the old Irish language is *Caillichin na Mochoirighe* which translates to Early-rising Little Hag.[12] The Hag is also associated with Bóinn.[13] So, the Hag and the Little Hag maybe the two stones of Rockabill Island. The hag has also been associated with stones such as The Cailleach Beara in Cork and The Cailleach Seat in the Loughcrew stone monument. Here again we see the connection with women and stones.

Helen Benigni maintains that there are three celestial bodies that guide us through our own Mythological cycles – the Sun, the Moon and Venus. It is these three celestial bodies that keep time for us and direct us to be in tune with the larger cycles of our lives.[14]

Rockabill Reflection:

Personal: I want the Sun, the heat the warmth to be balanced in my life. To be able to express my anger and my passions in a way that is healthy and healing. I want to be able to be in and with the darkness too.

Planetary: As humans we are overheating the planet. Bush fires in Australia and forest fires in the United States. Soaring summertime high temperatures all over the planet are killing us. Just like we need to personally balance our internal fire, we as humanity need to reverse the fire that is destroying us.

PART FOUR: AIR

*"It is said they raised a great wind, a Sídhe Gaoithe,
and the Danann came in through the air."*

Chapter Eighteen: Áed and the Tuatha Dé Danann

The final character in the story of Rockabill is a bit of a mystery. His name is Áed. I discovered just a very brief mention of him that led me to a much deeper unveiling of the importance of Rockabill as a sacred site of the Sídhe. It is said that the Tuatha Dé Danann came to Ireland from the air. Air is the element that is most associated with the Sídhe. They come in the air, through a mist or by the Sídhe Gaoithe, the Sídhe Winds. Below is the story of Áed.

One of the most famous High Kings of Ireland was Conn Cetchathach or Conn of the Hundred battles. Conn is said to have reigned between c120-140AD. The Lia Fail stone in Tara was said to roar with joy when the true High King of Ireland put his feet upon it, and it is said that it did so for Conn[1].

I will not list the hundred battles. However, there was one specific battle in the taking of Maigh Léine with the King of Ulster that left Conn and his army hurt and wounded. Then came unto him powerful friends of the Tuatha Dé Danann – Áed of Sith Dabhilla. Others that came were Áed of Eadar (now Howth), Criomhtann of Callain, Dearg of Sith Dearg and Aenghus of the Brugh. They brought with them curing plants for the lacerations, cuts and wounds, and healing herbs for their sores, so that Conn and his champions were made brave and smooth bodied at rising time on the following day. Of this Mythical person (Áed of Dabhilla), we know nothing, but Sith Dabhilla must be Cnoc Dabhilla now Abill Rocks between Rush and Holmpatrick."[2]

There are several interesting facts in this story. One, it references

Áed of Sith Dabhilla and Aenghus of the Brugh as they had come together to help Conn. I have extensively researched all the persons called Áed that I could find in the literature and have narrowed it down to three. The name Áed means 'fire' or 'spark.' This again could be a link to the Sun God Áed. The segment also implies that Áed was a contemporary, friend or relative of Aengus of Brugh na Boinne, who was the son of Bóinn, who we met in an earlier chapter. This passage in the translation tells us that Áed was of the Tuatha Dé Danann. We know from previous writings that Aengus had a brother called Áed, that is one of the possibilities for who this Áed was.

At the time when the Spanish Milesians came to conquer the Tuatha Dé Danann and take over the Country they were said to have retreated into the Otherworld. The Dagda, their High King, made a distribution of all such palaces in his kingdom.[3] Maybe the Dagda allocated Áed his kingdom on Cnoc Dabhilla?

Although O'Curry has said we know nothing of the Áed of Sith Dabhilla, we can make some assumptions from what small pieces that have been written in the manuscripts.

Dr Alexandra Koltypin talks about the nature of the Tuatha Dé Danann. This description is very much like the qualities that Áed and his compatriots have as members of this special tribe:

"They were a scientific people who comprehended the laws of nature and were able to operate them. The Tuatha Dé Danann had all around knowledge of the curative and power properties of plants and used them for treatment of the various diseases, mortal wounds and for the commissioning of spells. They also were very skilful handicraftsmen and musicians, soldiers and poets, and their weapons were considered as the best and modern. Women had almost the same civil rights as men, and actively participated in all men's affairs, even in war. Quite often they spoke as envoys at negotiations between the conflicting

parties, and sat at councils at the conclusion of peace."[4]

What I found most interesting about this small piece about Áed was that he and his friends of the Tuatha Dé Danann did not come as re-enforcements to help Conn fight. They came to help, to heal and to give succour to their friends.

Chapter Nineteen: Sith Dabhilla

What is the signification of 'Sith' Dabhilla? The word Sid, Sidh or Sith can be applied directly to the people associated with the mounds, such as Newgrange, Knowth and Dowth, as well as to the mounds themselves.[5] Sith or Sídhe can also be a word that is used to describe the 'Otherworld.' Wentz tells us that the Celtic Otherworld is located in the Ocean.[6] It is a place whose entrance is often described as an island out to sea, an ancient mound, or a bog.[7] It is clear from the writings that the people of the Sídhe and the places they inhabit are also called Sídhe and are in remote sacred spots. Carey states that the islands are in the East and that otherworldly beings live there underground.[8]

Many sacred and hidden places are said to be connected to the Sídhe all over Ireland. Some believe that they are Fairy Folk who went underground after the takeover of Ireland. The word Fairy comes from 'The Fair Folk,' which could allude to their fairness or brightness, as they are also said to be very tall people with a glowing and shimmering translucent quality. This description is given of them by a mystic:

"... those which are opalescent and seem lit up by a light within themselves. ... there was first a dazzle of light, and then I saw this came from the heart of a tall figure with a body apparently shaped out of half transparent or opalescent air, and throughout the body ran a radiant, electrical fire, to which the heart seemed the centre. I then thought that I had visions of Aengus, Manannan, Lugh, and other famous kings and princes of the Tuatha Dé Danann." [9]

The fact that there was a Sidh on Rockabill is very significant in my view. There may have been ancient monuments on Rockabill thousands of years ago but that would be nearly impossible to be proven now as there is a lighthouse on the site. I believe that the Tuatha Dé Danann knew of the significance of Rockabill and when they did retreat to the Otherworld, this was a place that they considered to be a Sith.

The fairy lore is held ancient and sacred in this Country. One of the most recent ones was the changing of the motorway in Co Clare so as not to disturb a fairy tree. This event was led by Eddie Lenihan a famous Folklorist who has accumulated a book of stories all about the Sídhe called *Meeting the Other Crowd*. Eddie says, "Because the fairies in Ireland are not a vague, impersonal force, they are people like us. Of a different a parallel word, maybe, but like us in enough ways to be understood by us sufficiently to make us wary of them, respectful of their habitation." [10]

The Rock and The Sídhe

White quartz and the Sídhe are also linked in folklore. In some of the legends written about Donegal, it is said that there were never white quartz stones anywhere but a place where the hill folk had a dwelling. They were considered fairy stones by right. [11]

The fact that Rockabill is made exclusively from white quartz and is linked with the Sídhe is in my view another piece of ancient Mythology that shows the significance of Rockabill.

As I previously said, Áed means 'fire' or 'spark.' We know that Aenghus was a Sun God too. The story of *The Return of the New Sun*, where Aenghus replaces the Dagda as the Sun God in Newgrange at the Winter Solstice, is one of the main stories in Irish Mythology. Is Áed the Sun God a reference to the sun rising over Rockabill on the Winter Solstice too?

The Tuatha Dé Danann were thought to seek refuge where no eyes could see them in Tír Fo Thuinn (Land Under the Wave)[8] and that they became small and elven or fairy-like. Others say that they are tall wise ethereal people beings.[9]

Is Rockabill a home of the Sídhe? This question can probably never be answered for many reasons. There is currently a renewed interest in many instances of different people from different countries having some interactions and communications with the Sídhe. They believe that the Sídhe are making themselves known again and communicating with some individuals. The English writer and Mystic, John Matthews, is one such writer and has detailed his communications with the Sídhe in a passage grave in Ireland which held a stone glyph, that when he meditated upon it, heard the voices of the Sídhe and wrote extensively about it.[11]

When I read this, the hairs on my arms stood up and I wondered why. Since I read the John Matthews book, I have had an overwhelming, compelling sense to write about Rockabill. I did have a strong sense of a 'calling' from somewhere to write about it. A sense of something hidden that wanted to be revealed – that is the only way I can explain it. I began to have what I describe as 'waking dreams' every time I thought about Rockabill and maybe one of the reasons why I could not bring myself to write a 'factual' book, so to speak.

Chapter Twenty: Connecting with the Sídhe

I do feel that there are some magical, mystical and mysterious happenings about. Every time I think of these wonderful beings, a sense of magic and mystery surrounds me. They certainly are 'light' beings and every time I connect or think of them (this feels the same somehow), I feel I huge sense of the lightness of my own being. It is funny and even paradoxical that I have discovered how light I really am through stone!!

It is like losing a part of yourself, then finding it again somehow. I even find it very difficult to explain how it feels for me. I have resisted the call of the Sídhe for a long time. It was a vague sense of something that was a gentle prompt and now it feels like a loud but still easy roar, like they are saying, "Talk to us. We need you to connect, to reconnect." The word 'merging' keeps coming into my head when I think of the Sídhe. It is like they are wanting to merge with us, and we only need to open ourselves up to this willingness to connect and it will happen.

Because of our human bodies and our heaviness of being, we are either anchored in the physical, or alternatively when we connect with spirit we get anchored into the spiritual.

Bringing the spiritual into the physical – this, I think, is our quest. In esoteric philosophy it is known as the dawning of the seventh ray of light.

The Seventh Ray

According to this philosophy the seven rays of light permeate everything. The cosmos, the universe, the planets, humans, and all other species too. Some rays are dominant, and others are not and they come in and out of importance at different times.

From a spiritual perspective, humanity is moving from a sixth ray influence into a seventh ray influence. The sixth ray would view Source as above and external; it creates devotion to a single individual like Jesus, Mohammad, Buddha, etc. Whereas the seventh ray would view Source as more internal within us and needs to be grounded in the physical. Source is in everything. This seventh ray feels more like Animism in the sense that it sees Spirit in everything.

At the cusp of the transition, there are many problems for us currently as humans. Sometimes we cannot see the bigger picture.

The Sídhe are deeply affected by this also. They are beings of light and the merging of their light with our physicality is coinciding with the bringing in or down of the seventh ray of existence. We need to help each other to do this. It is a stage in our evolution that will take time. My vision is that when we ask the Sídhe to come to us, they do and when we look to Rockabill and places like it (powerful portal places) that have their strong energy within, and it will be easier to do.

This message of connection or indeed reconnection is a powerful one. Every time I think about Rockabill now, I can feel and sense the presence of the Sídhe, and their wonderful wisdom is calling out to me in a way that I find difficult not to respond to. I know in doing so, there will be a lot of people who will think that this is hocus pocus – as I probably would have myself a long time ago. However, since humans have been on this planet, they have had some form of communication with the subtle world. They have also, in most indigenous societies, known that the life force or spirit is in everyone solid and seen, as well as everything soft and unseen.

Chapter Twenty-One: The Sídhe Speak

I find that I need to go to a very light place in my being to be able to connect with the Sídhe. The breath is a good place to begin. I feel they speak through the breath rather than through the head, or the words seems more authentic when they are given through the breath. I feel they really want to share and connect with us as human beings and them as Sídhe beings.

I feel the Sídhe beginning to speak at this point. I say to this presence that I want the chapter to be a collaboration, not just me speaking but you and me speaking – us. Our voices blending and harmonising.

Me: I feel you want me to talk about your healing aspects, these healing abilities of your nature. What can you do to help us heal?

Sídhe: *Using our voices to heal. This is one of the most useful ways of healing, with toning, murmurings, singing, chanting, enchantments.*

Let our presence flow through you. Let our etheric selves lighten your physical selves. Love every cell of your being and this will help you heal. When you anger, you let the etheric darken, this is why you dislike anger so much – you remember your Sídhe nature and want to turn it into lightness and love.

Me: If I was to ask how do we co-operate with you more, what kind of things do we need to do?

Sídhe: *Become lightened in yourselves, feel the lightness of your* *etheric substance. This will help you feel the way we feel. It will start to help the co-operation. When you sense your own etheric nature, you will begin to sense ours. We are air, we are air form. Our thoughtforms are what you might call breezier than yours. The wind is the best way to catch a passing sense of us. These are two things you can start to do to connect.*

I received this personal message that I want to share with you:

Patricia, let go of your density. Your physical body is connecting and identifying with the pain body too much. You need to leave it behind and connect to the light body more, be in the air while still on the ground like your seven ray teachings. They are very wise, so listen to their wisdom and dance and sing. You are getting promptings to do this, so listen to them and heed the call when it comes.

When I received this message, you have no idea how appropriate it is to me. Dancing is something I love to do and the only exercise I love. Singing is also one of my first loves and brings me to a place of connection with everything. I need to heed this message, which I ignore a lot.

Sídhespeak

While writing, I felt the presence of an old man called Awen. He was a Merlin-type figure with long white hair and thin with a white beard. I can still see him very clearly and it was like he was dictating information to me – that is the only way I can explain it. I have transcribed word for word below what I said and how he answered.

Me: What is the significance of Áed?

Sídhe: *Áed means 'spark' or 'sun' and we are the people of the Sun, the Central Sun, the Sun behind the Sun. Some of us have come from* the stars too and we knew there would be a time when we would have to open communications with the human populations. This is needed to fulfil our role of making the earth purer. It is needed more now than it ever was or has been. Reverence for the planet, of all life on this planet is missing. We need to put the missing piece back into life. Our life, your life.

Me: How do we do this?

Sídhe: *There are many ways we can do this together, but not everyone will be open to our ways and will have the degree of openness or oneness to do it. Many are called but few are chosen, we believe that you know this phrase. One way we can raise the vibration of your part of the Earth is to meditate on the ground. Connect with your feet, connect with your head. Let the energies of the higher head drop down to the ground and into the Earth, this will help. They bring the energy of the Central Sun at the core of the earth into your feet, through your body and out into your environment. Develop these practices weekly then daily and you will see results.*

Me: In what way would you like me to portray you in the book I am writing?

Sídhe: *We are physical beings with much spirit included in our energy system. Some people may see us, hear us or feel us. You can hear us as your gift is clairaudience, which is why we are speaking through you at this time. We want people to know it is very rare that we do this. It is time now; it is time now that we work together as beings that can affect the changing nature of the planet for both our benefits.*

Me: How can we help that? What do we do?

Sídhe: *We can meditate together; you can call on us in your meditations and we can strengthen your requests. The sacredness of all things is what is the most important thing right now. Humans have lost this knowledge. The reason you are so connected to the stones is* *that they are speaking to you to go back to the ways of reverence for the planet. There will always be wars and conflict in this World of yours but there are ways to eliminate the overindulgence of humanity if you regain your reverence. This should be a slogan for you – "Regain your Reverence" – a saying for these times.*

What is it that I am hearing? My own inner voice? All I can say is that it was me, and not me. The words flowed onto the paper, and they are not the usual way I would speak. Is this channelling? Well maybe, but we channel all the time. When we paint, write, or partake in any form of creativity, we are channelling from somewhere. All I do know is that these communications have given me a sense of grace and reverence for the planet, the land, the stones, and all of life. It has made my life a more sacred one.

The Call of the Sídhe

Since I read that piece of Irish Mythology that states that Rockabill was a place of the Sídhe, of Áed, I have had a strong feeling of being pulled or drawn to speak about the Sídhe. When this happens to me, I tend to go straight into science and linear mode first and start researching and seeing what others are saying about this subject. It turns out some people are saying a lot. I always viewed the Sídhe as small fairy like creatures that you do not mess with. The tree spirits, the fairies at the forts, the garden gnomes and anything and everything in between.

Some believe that they are the spirit of the ancient Tuatha Dé Danann who went underground after the conquering of Ireland by the Milesians. The origins of the Sídhe are disputed. Some say they came in a wind from the North maybe from some of the Nordic lands into Ireland. Another theory is that they came down from the clouds in a mist, maybe originating from the stars. Wherever they have originated from, they seem to be communicating with humanity at this time. Works by John Matthews, David Spangler and Soren Hauge have all alluded to the voice of the Sídhe, in these times we are living through now.

Sídhespeak message I received on 01/03/22

"I am the overseer of the Sídhe in your place. You are pure of heart, Patricia. This is why we want to speak through you. We have important messages to give to Humanity at this crisis hour. Muri-el is my name and I know you want to connect with the feminine aspect of us. Although we do not see ourselves in the polarity that you do in your humanness. We need to unite as one species so we can overcome the badness and evil on the Earth at this time. The more people who know about us and can tune in and communicate with us, this will be for the benefit of everyone. We have stayed here on Earth to infuse your planet with our sacred thoughts and our reverence for you and the Earth. We know the pain you are going through and we hope that the goodness of most people on Earth will win out. There is a plan, and we hope the balance will be tipped in Earth's favour. Tune into the stones as you have done for the last number of years. Your soul knows the meaning of the stones, that is why they are calling you. The purity of the crystals will help you. Come visit us, we are waiting for you.

Sídhe Speak 19/07/2022

I felt a tingle at the top of my head. Looking at the chapters of my book, I got a strong feeling and an inner voice that said, "Let us speak. Let us do the talking for a while."

Me: What do you want to say at this time?

Sídhe: *We just want to come and let you know we are here to help you.*

131

Me: Do you mean with the book writing?

Sídhe: *Yes, to assist you in telling people about us in a way that they will understand.*

Me: Is it your general presence or at Rockabill (Dabhilla)?

Sídhe: *Both really. You have tapped into the Sídhe magic at Rockabill, and we want to share some of it with you.*

Me: What do you mean by magic?

Sídhe: *The magic of the World, the elements, the things you take so much for granted that we see as our vitality. We lack the solidity of you. This is why we are here. You have written about the solidness of the rocks, the groundedness of the stones. We do not have that solidity and the rocks provide it for us.*

Me: Wow, that is so interesting. I personally do not have that solidity either I am all in my head and find living in a body very difficult. Is this lack of solidity a problem for the Sídhe?

Sídhe: *Not a problem as such, just an awareness of it. We are always near places that have this solidity, they also have energy points too. You are right about that. They will be places that are solid and strong but have not been too overrun with human activity.*

Me: How can I be of service to the Sídhe in my writing?

Sídhe: *We want you to come to the stones and be with us, connect with us and write what you experience. You had a meditation that was very close to what is here, the crystal portal.**

It does not need to be physically seen. It is in the ether where we mostly reside. We do use the vibrational energy of the crystal quartz to charge our being and you can do this too.

---

* In the chapter on Spirit I tell of my experience of going to the Crystal Portal on Rockabill

Me: Can I be healed by the stones and how would this happen?

Sídhe: *It happens both physically and energetically. You set an intention of healing and when you come to sit on the stones, we can come and help with the healing process.*

Me: When is the best time to come?

Sídhe: *When the sun is low and birds have flown and you feel a sense of rightness. All the elements need to be there. Sun, water, wind and of course the stones of the Earth.*

Me: Thank you so much for speaking with me today. Are there any other words you would like me to transmit?

Sídhe: *We are the Sídhe Gaoithe, the Sídhe of the wind. Our presence is felt by listening to the voice of us in the wind, the spark on your window, the sensations in your body. We have much to learn from each other and we hope this will be the start of a beautiful co-creation.*

Me: Blessings and thanks to you.

Communication

This is the way that we can communicate with the Sídhe beings. It does not always have to be about, "What do I need to do?" This is an important question but like any relationship it needs to be developed and there is a need to get to know each other. There is a type of momentum to the communications that I am having with the Sídhe and they are gently encouraging me to begin to have a more frequent communication with them.

My sense of how to do it is this… You close your eyes, and you breathe gently and let the breath settle. You put your focus on the area of your heart, just about the heart chakra (at the breastbone), where you point with your hand to say, "Me."

Focus your consciousness on this area. Call to the Sídhe, with a verse like:

"Sídhe, Sídhe, please come to me.

Fae, Fae, come this way."

Whatever few words resonate with you. And make it rhythmic and musical if you can.

Put your consciousness on your heart area and listen. Their presence is felt or not felt by everyone very differently, as we are all so different. However, they say at a soul level we are all the same, so there will be some form of transfer of energy or soul to soul contact if you do so in an open and innocent way. Have no expectations and let it happen. Sometimes it will and sometimes it won't. Have a piece of paper nearby to record what has taken place and again it may be a picture, a few words, a sense of something but know that the Sídhe are here, they want to communicate with us and they want to partner with us to help the planet.

This is why they are seeking us out at this time. It is a time of crisis, and they want us to join together to help the situation that we face as a race.

I want to come into partnership with the Sídhe beings that I feel are calling me. It is a misty kind of relationship now. I feel there is a way that I can do this that will involve me and singing, I need to connect not through mind but through an inner voice, my untamed and free voice. The freer I feel, the freer I will be to connect with the Sídhe. If I can remove all the heaviness of thought forms that cloud my ability to be able to connect at a partnership level with the Sídhe, this is what I need to do. To blow away all the murky mucus-based thinking and just be my essential self, my essence. Then they will feel it easier to approach me. That is my sense of it.

Sídhespeak 29/08/22

Sídhe: *Don't deny or try to fight the fact that we are speaking through you, Patricia. We are. We are. We are one, we are the same essence as you. Our outer form is so different, but our souls match vibrationally.*

So, creating a 'soulspeak' way of connecting is what is best to do. Go inside your vast potential whatever way feels best for you and then call on us using our Sídhe names if you have them. We will come and we will share and we will befriend. It is time to do this now for the sake of humanity and the planet. We have investment in this planet just like you do. Our places of solace are being threatened too by your ways of using up the resources. This will all come to no good, you know it and we know it.

We think if we can communicate with you, this will have a positive impact. We are afraid that our purity will be compromised with more connection, but we see no other way. We need to understand your heaviness and you need to understand our lightness. We can have a positive impact on each other this way.

Me: What about this Sirius connection, is that important now?

Sídhe: *You know we all hail or have our origins from the various stars that are in our universe. Sirius is one of those stars. It is important because it can be seen from the Earth, and it is a very bright star. The connection that you have made between Dabhilla and the Dog Star is accurate. However, the real message behind all this is that all substance whatever it is, is sacred. Stars, stones, humans, Sídhe, plants, animals we all have a spark of the Source inside us, and we need to begin to see this in everything. This is the challenge. Come help us.*

Me: What can I personally do to help this?

135

It will be to write about it in your book. We will ensure that whoever needs to read it will do so and sense its importance. They may be a chosen few or indeed a chosen many. This does not matter. It is matter that matters. It needs to matter to you and all of humanity at this time.

Me: Can you help us see how we need to change our ways?

We are a portal to the world we need to create. We need to do this in a partnership sort of way. It has to be based on equality. The word Alliance has been used and it is the best word for what needs to happen between Human and Sídhe. If we can understand more about you, and you understand more about us, we can help each other to birth a new type of Earth. This is the challenge, and we can begin it here and now.

Healing

When I turned forty, I began to have a huge interest in healing. I don't really know why it was. I felt a deep need to heal myself and wanted to heal others. I remember signing up for a spiritual healing course.

When the trainer asked why we were here, all the other women knew why they were there. They had practices of various kinds and wanted to add healing to their work. It came to me, and I just said, "I don't really know why I am here. I just feel very drawn to healing." At the time I was working as a Health Education Officer which had nothing really to do with healing.

I am on a writing retreat, and I am trying to put together a draft for this book. I feel the need to ask about healing and the Sídhe. The theme of healing keeps coming up for me personally but also the healing nature of the Sídhe and the healing that needs to happen between Humanity and the Sídhe. So I begin to attune and ask about this again

Healing and the Sídhe 15/10/22

Me: What do we need to heal in relation to each other – our relationship with each other?

Sídhe: *There are many things that need to be healed. As of now, our planetary places are being invaded and this is what is troubling us. It may be a case we need to restate which we do not want to do. We share this Earth with you and do not want to abandon it. We have a message for you about this planet. We cannot stress enough that you MUST change your relationship with it. It has to be seen as sacred, as sacred as any church, as any sacred place that you can think of. Sacred means special or holy or separate whatever words you want to use. This is the immanent message; this is the most pressing message that we need to get across at this time.*

Me: If we heal our relationship to the Earth will this affect our relationship with the Sídhe?

Sídhe: *It will have that impact. We will be able to commune with each other again, if you can see how fragile we all are. Your etheric body is outside your physical body. When we retreated into the Earth, our physical body retreated also and we became etheric, so if you can tune into the ether, the air, you can attune to us, and we will become as one again. Separate but together in essence.*

Me: I feel a fear around being judged or being seen as mad having these conversations with invisible beings, how do I ignore these fears?

Sídhe: *Breathe into them. We understand your fears. Many stories have flourished in this World about us. Many are accurate but some are not. You have limitations and so do we. No-one is any more special than anyone else in our world. It is very different in your world with fame and humans who are well known and do many good things as you see it. We are not the same, no one Sídhe being is any better than* *any other. If there are lessons to learn, we all learn them, that is our way. So, you need to understand that you are no better or worse than any other human. Your fear is around what might happen after this communication, is that right?*

Me: Yes exactly – how I will be perceived.

Sídhe: *This is an ego thing. Your soul would not ask that question. You need to go to a soul place and decide does my soul care? Does my spirit care? What will be impacted will be your personality, your mind, your body possibly. Your essence will not care, so tune into this. – We are leaving now.*

Loss

I find it impossible to comment on any of the above, I am at a loss. At one level it feels mind blowing, at another the most natural thing in the World. I suppose I can leave any comments up to You the Reader to see if any of the information resonates with you. I do think these words contain some great insights and wisdom. I did get a bit personal, asking about myself, but I decided to leave those questions in the book, as it might be what any of you might also have asked.

Rockabill Reflection:

Personal: I feel the air in my lungs, I look up at the sky and see the air all around me. I need to listen to the Sídhe winds to connect with their voice in my own life and listen and act on the wisdom they impart. "With every breath I take, I release control and know another one will be there to breathe again."

Planetary: I believe a reconnection with the Sídhe beings is much needed in our world today. The Shining Ones can make us see the shining light within ourselves. Although there are places all over the planet that they have a distinct presence, here in Ireland, they seem to be embedded in the landscape. We can connect with them when and wherever we want. I feel if we do this, the great divide can be unified.

PART FIVE: SPIRIT

"We are spirits in a material World."

Sting

Chapter Twenty-Two: Feminine Freedom

I have felt a huge separation with what is known as the Divine Feminine. I was brought up in the Catholic faith which saw God, Jesus, and the Holy Spirit as male. I remember at a young age having a distinct feeling of being 'left out' of religion and spirituality.

The church ruled our daily lives in a lot of ways in the 1970s. My mother was the church organist and me and my siblings sang in the choir. There was always Sunday masses, Holy days, Holy festivals, May and October devotions, Men's and Women's sodality. I did not even know what any of them were for. All I remember was that the priests ruled, and they were all men.

Women played very minor roles and they were either virgins or whores. The two Marys, Jesus Mother or Mary Magdalene. This polarity of representation of the two most important women was a great concern for me. Is it any wonder I rejected it?

There is still a huge gap in the female representation of women in all the major religions and it is an area that I think needs to be transformed. I like the idea that the ultimate God energy, Source, whatever word for Spirit that fits, is genderless. I love the idea of having the freedom to express my spirituality in whatever way I want to and not be restricted by specific dogmas or set of rules. I find religious dogma very restrictive, as it does not encompass every person. I find it polarising – you are in or you are out, we are the right religion, they are the wrong one, kind of idea. I find it breeds separateness, not oneness. That is how it is for me anyway.

Spirit can show up in many forms in the World. I have always struggled with seeing spirit through physical things like the landscape. The spirit of Rockabill is in the material it is composed of, but also in the way it can evoke spirit within a person.

Freedom has been an important theme running through this book. This chapter is no different. While looking for freedom from the restrictions of my body and my mind, I am also looking for Spiritual Freedom. The heaviness I sometimes feel in my body can be reflected in my spirit also. It may be related to karma or the other way of explaining it can be life lessons that I do not learn. The belief that I have in relation to past lives obviously informs this to a great extent. To me it is not just a pie in the sky belief, it makes much more sense to me as a way of giving meaning to life. It is cyclical and evolutionary, like all the rest of life on this planet.

I think we incarnate into a lifetime that gives us the potential to learn certain lessons and this happens until we have learned all the lessons and then we are removed from the wheel of rebirth and can go off into the spiritual sunset and float on by! Well, it makes just as much sense as going to Heaven and doing whatever they do there. Who really knows what happens in the 'other' reality?

Escaping

There is something about trying to always get away from something, even in my spiritual life.

Trying to escape – move from one state of being to another. I have used many different methods to do this. Back in my youth it was prayer groups. I became involved with the charismatic renewal movement. I was a teenager, I did not know which way was up to be honest, it was the singing that I enjoyed most. Looking back, it was a movement that moved through me and came out the other side. There were moments of great fellowship and connection with Spirit, but it was a Catholic-based belief which I did grow out of as time passed. Mainly because of the lack of any women at the core of the religion, or any major religion for that matter. It did make me realise that I did need and want to have a spiritual dimension to my life.

There was a bit of a hiatus in my twenties, as I was married at aged twenty-two and immediately had babies. Spirit did not really come into my life at this stage as I was so busy in the material world.

After my car accident in 1996, I was given a book called *Conversations with God* by Neale Donald Walshe. It was at the time something of a controversial book, but I absolutely loved it. Here was a man on the brinks of ending his life and he asked or pleaded or demanded from God to hear him or answer him and what emerged was a series of books about what God said to him. Books have played a huge part in my spiritual life too.

Chapter Twenty-Three: A New Age

I have always had a disregard for labels. New Ageism is one of them. I believe that the New Age we are living in is a very exciting one in terms of Spirituality. Some say it is the move from a Piscean Age to an Aquarian Age, from an astrological perspective. If you ascribe to this belief, then it is a new age. For me it is about freedom. These times allow you to explore spirituality but not in a dogmatic or religious way. We can make our own minds up. We are not hemmed in by the rules and regulations of a dogma or of a specific religion. We have moral rules and if you follow a particular form of spirituality there are ways of practicing that.

I remember for a long time I was very caught up with wanting to know my life purpose. Why am I here? What is the purpose of my life? I think I have had different purposes at different times. So being a mother was one that was definitely on the list. When my role as a mother was not as all-consuming and as I began to have more 'physical' freedom as my children grew up, I started to pursue my spiritual life in a deeper way. I was looking for another spiritual purpose.

Is it my soul calling me to write about Rockabill? If it was only my brain, my mind, and my body I would have thrown in the towel long since. It is like that higher part of my nature wants this story to be seen and heard. I can only liken it to a voice in your head that won't let go and is holding on to you, whispering to you and waiting for you to make your moves.

We might then ask, what is the soul? What is that spirit essence, that part of you that is guiding you to be true to your soul's calling? There have been many times when I have questioned whether there was such a thing as soul.

This idea of a guiding light is interesting to me, and I was not sure about soul or spirit until a seemingly trivial event happened to me which changed my view. Here is the story:

I was on a double decker bus coming home from the city. I think I was about fourteen years old. At that time when you left the bus, it sometimes opened its door without pulling into the stop so it would actually stop on the motorway, and you would jump off. I stood up rang the bell and waited for the door to open. The driver stopped on the road and I went to jump off when a force that was so strong held me back, it was like a big invisible arm going across me preventing me from moving forward. I pushed and pushed but could not move. At the exact same time, this happened – a motorbike sped past the door of the bus at high speed. When it passed the force that was stopping me instantly left and I was able to jump off the bus. This all happened in a split second. Now when I say, "The force," it sounds a bit like a Star Wars scene. For me, that is exactly what it felt like.

I remember going to bed that night thinking about how I would have suffered a horrible death by being struck by a speeding motorbike. The incident always stayed with me, and I felt a sense that I was being directed by an invisible force, or Spirit or whatever you want to call it. It gave me a sense of being protected by something that is bigger than myself. I also remember feeling that maybe it was not my time to leave this earth and Spirit took over in that moment and prevented my early demise.

My belief now is that things like this happen to wake you up. It has happened to me a few times in my life and not always as dramatic or as nice as the event I have just told you about.

Sometimes it was sitting in the dark by myself thinking nobody understands the pain of grief or even just the pain of pain, when a chink of light comes through, fighting with your own thoughts in the hope that a good one will peer over the parapet and take over, and give you the sense of absolute joy when you erupt into a fit of laughter and cannot stop.

Chapter Twenty-Four: Visible versus Invisible

What does 'to be seen,' actually mean? We are seen everyday day by many people. Are we really seen? Is our inner life seen by everyone? No, it is not. This for me is what really being seen is about. When I think of writing this book, I think of how others will now know my innermost thoughts about myself and life. This is very disconcerting and yet I feel a compelling need to write about Rockabill and how it has impacted my life.

I remember during a really difficult time for me in my thirties, I did not want to be seen as attractive, so I ate and put on weight so I would not be attractive. I thought it was an unconscious thing and now that I am writing about it here, I realise I was taking up more space by being heavier. It was emotional eating because I was so unhappy in my job and with my life in general. I always let external events, people, or society dictate what I did. It was exhausting.

Living for Others

It is exhausting, always trying to live up to what you think others want. Whether it is society, your family, your work, yourself. I remember during the boom years in Ireland when we had the Celtic Tiger as I mentioned previously, I was very unhappy. I felt that we were all on this merry-go-round and I wanted to jump off but everyone around me was saying, "No – time to par-tay! Let's us go on a huge holiday. Let us get a new car. Let us buy a million-pound house," or whatever it was (I do not have a million-pound house by the way). I just felt that this new-found materialism was not in keeping with my inner yearnings.

It went against my spiritual life, and it felt like consumerism was the new religion. Material life was all that mattered – I felt there was a loss of soul in some respects at this time.

The stealing of the Glas Gablin came back into my mind, as Balor wanted all the plentifulness for himself.

There is always a huge gap between the visible and invisible worlds. Yet according to Esoteric Spirituality, we are coming under the seventh ray influence where we need to spiritualise matter. Maybe I was feeling that sense of, "Where is the Spirit in all of this?" Our visible lives need to have Spirit in them. Our spiritual lives need to have matter in them. One of the ways we must do this is by venerating the Earth, her body, our planet. She is the spiritual materialised.

The Sídhe are invisible beings – well to me, anyway. Some people have the gift of second sight and can physically see etheric or subtle beings. My gift is more about Clairaudience.

I can hear the voice of Spirit sometimes very loud, mostly very quietly. The messages are usually very lovingly directive and full of wisdom and love. They can speak in very different ways. A lot of the time, I get a sense of them wanting to speak to me and I ignore it. There is a part of me that is still disbelieving of what I am hearing. Is it me? Is it them? Is it my inner highest self?

Invisible Woman

There comes a time in a woman's life where she seems to become invisible. After a certain age, when physical attractive aspects begin to leave, (or what others see as attractive – mainly youthfulness), it can be replaced by a sense of, "Who am I, if I am not my body?" Here is the rub, the more I become invisible, the more I sense the visible in the World.

I think I have always sensed Spirit in my life in some form. I liken it to a voice within, a pull, an inner knowing that the source of your being is always calling in some way. Connecting with that source has happened in various way for me. It has up to this point, been about meditation of various kinds. At this stage it is connecting with the physical and seeing the spiritual in the physical.

Chapter Twenty-Five: The Seventh Ray – "The force that seeks to ground the spirit"

That Spirit, the force of life that is in everything and is everything. Sometimes we do not see how Spirit pervades all of life from a grain of sand to a planet – the life force that has created all life is in everything. This book is a call to all who seek to see that Spirit is in everything. I have experienced this in my connection with stones. Concretising Spirit to form. If we could do this, everything would be seen as sacred.

The seventh ray is also known as the Spirit of Restoration, a way to restore some of the ancient mysteries. The ancient mysteries of Rockabill and how it can be a portal of light for doing this in our lives today. It will create a synthesis, a unity, a oneness, so we will sense that oneness in everything we do and see.

To love with your mind, now there is something to challenge!! I would always have associated love with the emotional body, the seventh ray will bring mind and heart into the equation. May the highest and the lowest meet, this is the seed thought of the ray. To quote one of my spiritual teachers to, "Reach for the stars but keep your feet on the ground."

Below is an extract from a conference I recently attended regarding bringing in the seventh ray. It was given by William Meader, an American teacher of the Ageless Wisdom Philosophy.

Another aspect of the seventh ray is the importance of ritual. Using ritual to invoke devic life. The goal of Humanity is to co-operate with the devas. Devas in Sanskrit means 'Shining Ones.' This seventh ray is bringing in the consciousness of the devas. The higher your consciousness, the higher devic life you can connect and co-operate with. Your etheric substance holds the Angelic (devic) energy. Our solar angels are bringing in the mind too.

I have experienced this connection with the Sídhe through a ritual practice. It is also very interesting that the Tuatha Dé Danann are known as 'The Shining Ones'!! Sanskrit is the oldest form of writing in the World, so the name Shining Ones is an ancient name.

Chapter Twenty-Six: Becoming a Yogi

I am on a book writing retreat in Co Wicklow and looking forward to doing some writing and meeting new people. There is a very small book shop attached to it and I wander in, as I always do to book shops. I had nothing in mind to buy at all, when on the shelf I see a book called *Autobiography of a Yogi* by Paramahansa Yogananda. It is a very famous book about how he brought Kriya Yoga to the West. I had been wanting to read it for a long time, as it was mentioned in a lot of books I had recently been reading, telling me that Kriya Yoga was the 'aeroplane' method to the God experience.

I looked around the shop for something else to catch my attention, but it didn't. I knew I was going to buy it and start to read it that night, so I gave in and bought it. I had a room on my own which I always delight in as I have shared a room with others my whole life. I settled into bed and opened the first page. Suddenly, or maybe very gently, I can't really remember, the room began to fill will the most beautiful smell of flowers. I looked around – had I left a candle burning, was there a soap nearby? – nothing. I felt a presence of something, I cannot say what that was, but it was palpable in the room that night. It was also sweet, gentle and heart-warming – that is the only way I can explain it. I became more intrigued with this Kriya that Yogananda was talking about. Now if you don't believe in randomness or synchronicity the next bit is a bit of a head wreck. There was a lovely big notice board in the retreat centre and at the lunch break I went over to have a look at all the holistic notices. This plain white notice caught my eye. A master of Kriya Yoga was coming to Ireland to talk about Kriya and to initiate people into the path, and this man was in the same lineage as Yogananda. This was Wednesday and he was coming on Friday, two days later. I could not get it out of my head, am I supposed to do this? Will I go from one retreat to another, will my husband be a bit peeved that I am extending my week's break for another few days? I rang the number and the woman on the other end said yes there is one place left. So I booked it and there I was going to something I did not really know what or where it might lead, but knowing it was something that I was really meant to do.

This second retreat centre was in Co Meath, and I wandered into the room and met two of the most lovely women (Margaret and Dolores) who gave me a rundown on this spiritual master as they called him. They had been waiting to meet him for years. Did I realise who he was etc? I did not have a clue and thought to myself "what am I doing here? Despite this, I entered the room where he was sitting cross-legged looking like a grandfather and people were bowing to him. "Oh no," I thought. This reverence jarred with me, as I think everyone has a God spark in them and why are we bowing to him?!

I felt the old Catholic bias of blind reverence and male God coming back to haunt me, yet still something was pulling me to go with my intuition.

He spoke about Kriya and the power of it. His speech was translated into English by a lovely doctor who was his assistant. Despite myself, I felt a huge warmth and compassion emanating from this man. I had some profound spiritual experiences during that weekend. The relationship between a guru and a disciple is a very personal one, I find it difficult to explain it. All

I can say is that I knew that I was meant to be there at that time and to meet him.

He was offering initiation into the path of Kriya in Dublin the following week. We were to bring a donation, and small gift – some incense or fruit was what was usually given. I went to the initiation with about five other people. I began to practice the breathing exercises daily and weekly meet with the woman who organised the Kriya here in Ireland.

Then in 2010, I went to India to be given the second set of Kriya exercises. As they are very specific, powerful and potent exercises and you need to be shown by a master who knows them and who knows you very well. I spent nine nights in this Ashram just outside Kolkata. It was one of the most beautiful experiences I have ever had. The yoga, the people, the food. Everyone I met there seemed to be highly spiritual and I felt so loved and loving during that time, it was like being wrapped in unconditional love by the most loving mother and father. We went to Sri Yukteshwar's (another Kriya master of the same lineage) temple while there. And again, I had another deeply moving experience while meditating there.

When I returned home however, I found the next set of exercises very difficult to do physically. The breath work was painful on my mouth and holding my breath was painful on my body. I had to stop as it was making me have Fibromyalgia flare ups every time I meditated. They were very painful. I stopped going to the weekly meetings as the point was to do your practice which I could not do. In 2018, Guruji (my teacher) left his mortal body. A night or two after that I had a very vivid dream where he came to me and told me I was a 'Kriyabhan' in my heart and always will be. He said it did not matter if I could not do the exercises. I remember crying for hours afterwards. I miss my Kriya family dearly and I connect with some of them on Facebook from time to time and each one of them is a most beautiful soul.

I think that Yogananda brought the science of Kriya Yoga to the west, and it created a unity of the teachings of the east and the west. There is a union about it. I also felt that the path was a very masculine one, an idea that I sometimes struggle with. I see the imbalance of the feminine in a lot of spiritual paths. I think the message that I take from being a 'Kriyabhan' is that I need to rise above the identification of gender for in a world of pure spirit where we are all one.

Chapter Twenty-Seven:
"Why does the caged bird sing?"

When I was two years old, way back in 1963, I experienced a personal trauma that has resonance for me to this day. It was like any event that would happen to a small child and would probably have saved their life, but now would be treated so very differently than this.

I was out in a park with my family and while we were all piled into the car, I banged my head on the car door. As I lay in the back of the car, I fell asleep. Now I have been told this part of the story by others so I don't really know the exact details, but I think they were trying to wake me up and could not. My mother thought I was suffering from concussion and her and my father rushed me to the hospital.

The part I do remember is waking up on a hospital gurney, and seeing my mother, father and grandfather being whisked out of the hospital and me lying there not knowing what was going on. Of course, as a young child I began to cry, shake and wanted to get up. The medical staff then tied me to the gurney with straps. I remember feeling helpless, stuck and literally tied down, then everything went black. I presume they gave me a sedative or a mask to put me out or whatever.

Every now and then when I think of this, I realise how it has impacted on my life. If I ever feel that I am in a sticky situation, something that I cannot see a way out of, I feel trapped, stuck and frozen like a caged bird. I have re-lived through it in a therapeutic way so many times and now I can recall it without all the trauma attached. I do feel the sadness of it and try to remember all the people who have been caged, trapped, imprisoned in the many ways that can be and always feel a huge sense of empathy.

Singing has always played a huge part in my life. Born into a family of musicians, it has always been there in some shape or form. When I sing, I always feel a sense of freedom, my voice lifts up into the air, into the sky and is free. I sometimes wish my body would feel the same way. There are times when I feel trapped inside this body of mine.

Freedom and Healing

Feeling trapped and feeling free holds great meaning for me. Anything that I find constricting or controlling brings back horrible memories which sometimes I know I am not even aware of. I always feel that this story has played out in many other areas of my life. Whether I feel trapped in my body, trapped in an emotional rollercoaster of drama that is life, or feeling stuck in a materialist world that is so out of line with how I really want to be in this world, I feel trapped. I always want Spirit to come in and save me, take me away from all the hassle, to free me.

Going into a spiritual practice whatever it may be prayer, meditation, journeying, I seem to always use it as an escape mechanism. The truth that I have realised through writing this book is that we all have things we want to escape from.

I am my body; I am in my body; I don't need to escape from it. I am my thoughts; they are me. There is no need to get rid of them. I am my emotions; my passions and they are who I am. I am Spirit and soul too. The simple oneness of being. Sometimes our physical life will take over and need attention. Sometimes it may be the emotional life that is dominant. I always felt that when my spiritual life was to the forefront, and I meditated every day, that this was the most important. I now see that it all matters. It is all sacred and it is all about accepting and integrating. This is the healing that I have gone through.

The spiritual journey through life can be a funny one of many twists and turns and spiralling in and then spiralling out, of rocky roads and deep caverns. I find it kind of amusing that two rocks in my locality have led me to this place of healing and freedom. Maybe the stones have always been in my bones – I just did not realise it. The stability I needed to accept my spiritual path was leading me to the story of the rocks, it was there all the time, I was unaware of it.

Awareness is a good thing. Being able to see something that you previously could not, is a freeing experience. When you can see it or you realise it is there, you can do something about it. This journey to Rockabill that I have done, has taken me to places I did not know that were inside of me. The delight, the rage, the insights that it unleashed for me were eye-opening and transformative. The words 'healing' and freedom keep coming into my mind as I write this. I have experienced both of those in the process of discovering or even re-discovering the story of Rockabill and the story of my life through it. It has made me see the need for healing my emotions, my body, my relationships with others, whether they be human, Sídhe or Spirit beings.

The masculine and feminine aspects of us all whatever our leanings need to be integrated. I think I have integrated them more now. We all have these wounds that fester in our lives if we do not address them. Whatever they may be for us as individuals and collectively. One example of this is my own relationship to food was a symptom of not having enough and having a famine mentality and I realised that this was in my DNA of being an Irish person. Letting go of these things can be difficult. There is such freedom and healing in letting go. We may need others to help us, and we may do the work ourselves. And ultimately, when we do, our bones will hold us up, will give us strength and the wisdom to get through it all.

The famous Balor from the previous chapter had a daughter called Eithne or Eithnú. He kept her locked in a glass tower because of a prophesy that was told by a druid where Balor would be killed by his grandson. Balor did all in his power to keep Eithne locked up. Bóinn was also banished from the Well of Wisdom. These stories resonate so much with me because of the restrictions placed on the women in them. I think they shout out at me even more loudly because of the restrictions I have felt deeply in my own early experience as a child.

Chapter Twenty-Eight:
My Immram

One of my more recent spiritual experiences was an Iomramh or Immram spiritual journey.

I am doing a Shamanic training course and this journey was part of the course. It is a sea journey where you build a Currach (an old Irish boat) from your bones and then you go out to sea. When you return you are never the same. You have gone on a journey and you cannot go backwards only forwards. Two very famous Immrama in Ireland are *The Voyage of Bran* and *The Voyage of St Brendan*. Amantha Murphy in her book *The Way of The Seabhean*, tells us that an Immrama changes you. There is always a loss and a gain. The point is to let go of things that are restraining you. Allowing yourself to be free. You must ask yourself what you will bring back. Here is the journey I want to share with you as it feels so linked with Rockabill.

I went out to sea and my animal protector came with me which is a small white owl. This owl has been on a lot of Journeys. He was flying beside the Currach. I was pulled in by Bóinn onto Rockabill Island. I went deep into the Island and what I can only describe was a Crystal Palace stood before me. There were two Sídhe-like beings, one male and one female. They said they had a feast for me, and a big crystal screen appeared in front of me. It was like a movie of many different parts of my life on a large crystal screen. It showed the many traumas and difficulties that I had experienced in my life so far. I was told, "*Set your Stage, your light will shine through, be the authentic you. We are here to assist you always. It is about selfhood – simply be you.*"

I gave them a gift of my book, this book (which I have visualised a lot) – and they handed me a golden branch with a golden apple on it. Bóinn was with me throughout this process and then she said: *"With one foot in the sea, you are part of me. Be the Goddess you are meant to be. Stay humble, stay moist, drink of me."*

I have always tried to be an authentic person. If I am around someone and I sense that they are not being true to themselves, it does not feel right. If I am with someone and I seem to be behaving in a 'fake' way, this is something that really bothers me too. I try to see everyone as their essential selves as much as I can. This message was very clear. I know I can judge people and I have to keep constant vigilance about this. It can be a tough call at times.

The gifts they gave me I think relate to internal or second vision. I know W.B. Yeats wrote about the golden apples in a poem, so this is something I need to explore a bit more.

Rockabill Reflection:

Personal: I look back on my life and see how Spirit has shown up. Sometimes very dramatically sometimes very gently, to push me to a new level of awareness and sense of the spiritual essence in this lifetime of mine.

Planetary: At this time on our planet I see a huge gap between new world religions where there is a convergence, and old religions. Yet I also feel there is a change coming. We need to shed the old and make way for a new way, where all of humanity can begin to love one another regardless. It is an old call for a new way.

AFTERWORD

"The crane has a remarkable position in Celtic lore. The crane is believed to be the messenger of the gods and to have a high degree of wisdom. The crane represents higher states of consciousness."

Crane Wisdom

As I feel the end of the book approaching, I was wondering how to end it. It has gone from the deep wells, into rivers, oceans, rocks, the Sun, the sky and Spirit. Something was missing. Then the crane came back into my consciousness.

I have always noticed that when something comes into my head, it will not leave until I pay attention to it. There have been many times that this has not happened, where I dismiss it as unnecessary rumination and try to put it to the back of my mind and carry on. Sometimes it will not leave and keeps coming back for attention. This happened with the crane.

A few years ago, while walking out on the beach with Rockabill in sight, I spotted what I thought was a crane bird on a rock, so I stopped to look. The bird seemed to be looking at me too. Elegant, slim and tall, it continued to look at me until I broke away and then it flew in the direction of Rockabill. Now I realise that Crane birds have been extinct in Ireland for hundreds of years. What I saw was a heron. They apparently replaced the crane when it left way back when.

I could not stop thinking about crane birds. They were coming back into my mind again. So of course, I go online and read as much as I can about them and I still did not get the message of what the crane was saying to me, figuratively and symbolically, of course. I wrote the poem below in 2018 (I think) when my consciousness was obsessed with them.

Crane Mythos

(i)

In your sacred skin

Avian messenger to the Otherworld

Harbinger of Myth

Keeping secrets of the ancestors

Safe in your soft purr and garbled call

Your stringy legs spell out Ogham Alphabet

With sticks.

(ii)

Gods invoked you and danced

Corrghuineacht

Opening their other eye to see in

Between worlds

Goddesses revered you

Triple moon bird

Waxing full waning

Birth death rebirth.

(iii)

Shapeshifting

into Aoife

Then fading, dying

Leaving Manannan Mac Lir

So distraught he cut your skin

Into a crane bag

To hold you for eternity.

(iv)

Geranos

Your movements mirror

The Labyrinth

Winding

The way from conscious

To unconscious

This world to the underworld

And back again

Changed.

Cranes are deeply connected to Celtic Mythology, and they appear in some of the Mythological stories. They dance in circles in patterns of 3 and 9. Three is a number that is also connected to Irish Mythology. They are connected to wisdom and are said to be messengers of the gods.

The crane is also connected with the Cailleach and was called the Hag Bird. This was due to its shrieking call. I think I read somewhere that the meaning of Hag comes from *Haggios* which means wisdom. This word has been turned on its head and means old and ugly. What do older women have to do to get heard!!

It seems like a heralding of sorts to tell me that my book journey is ending. It is also just beginning. So there is birth, death and now it will be a rebirth of sorts, when it is read by you.

Of course, nothing is ever really complete, is it? I get the feeling the crane is trying to give me a message, but I am unclear about what it is? Being OK with being unclear is something that I used to really struggle with. I needed to see, to know what is ahead. Do we ever know what is ahead of us? One of my closest friend's daughter died very tragically as I was writing this book. She was thirty-seven years old. I knew her from a baby. It did not make any sense, and maybe there is no sense in it. Death is difficult whatever the circumstances. I think the message is something about the cycle of life. She left behind two young children. Her essence is with them, and they will carry her through their lives as will their children, if they have any.

Longevity is another trait of the crane bird. I always have the feeling I am going to die at age seventy-eight years old, I don't know why. Now there was a time when that was old, but now when women are living into their 90s, it seems young, and I am nearer to reaching that age now as I enter my sixties. Maybe I might extend it a bit further now! – seventy-eight seems way too close.

Death happens all the time. I remember when I had to give up work and was searching in the darkness for a meaning to my life, while not wanting it to be all about work. The 'role' you have, the job you do. "What do you do?" It is nearly always the first question that you ask someone when you meet them first.

This idea of always doing – we always must be 'doing' something. That Human Being versus Human Doing idea. I think it again is the balance between the two things. In this World, doing is a lot more valued than being. We have been doing for thousands of years. Maybe it is now time to be for a while.

Even though I thought the Covid pandemic was terrible and we lost many beautiful souls too early from Covid, it was also a time of stopping and giving the planet a chance to breathe. It reminded me so much of the human condition. One minute we are watching sea life come back into the oceans and even into city rivers, the next seeing so many people die in our hospitals.

Anything that is gone from us, that has left us, that has moved on is dead. I want to become more at home with death and I think that I will be able to love more as a result. I started this book talking about the womb, the birth the beginning, and ending it with death the end. However, it is not the end, but an ending and a moving on. I am sure my relationship with Rockabill will change as I get older. Now that I have told the story and got the wonderful ancient history of the rocks into written form, it is gone from my head into this book.

Recently there was an article about the return of the crane bird to Ireland. It has been gone for over three hundred years. Maybe this the herald, the return of crane wisdom is coming back also. Mary Pat Lynch in her wonderful article on *Women and Crane Myth* evokes the Crane Woman:

"Thus say the Crane Women: We live with arcane lore, secret knowledge, and contra-diction, the speaking of opposites. We love the edges, the fringes, the places where things grow and die. We ravel and unravel, where ideas from different places mix and merge. If you seek crane knowledge, learn patience. We are secretive and do not volunteer what we know. The deepest answers come only to the skilful questioner." [1]

One of the qualities associated with the crane is patience. I have frequently asked myself why I did not know about the Rockabill story earlier in my life. I would have had more energy to share my writing. I would have been able to do more activities to promote the story. I think the Crane is teaching me that this was not the case. I needed the experiences I have had to share with people. It is only when you get to a 'certain' age that you have the wisdom to know this. I think I know it now. There is a time for everything to happen and we need the patience for it to happen at a time when it is right.

The crane can also herald a transition to the Otherworld. Now I do not think that I am going to die soon (not yet anyway). Instead, I am interpreting this as a message to accept the wisdom and knowledge that I have gained about the existence of the Otherworld.

The crane has been associated with stones in history. Aristotle described how the cranes carried a touchstone inside of them and it was used to test gold when vomited up. Pliny wrote that a crane would hold a stone in its claw as it fell asleep and would drop it when it awakened.[2] It was known as a herald of sorts.

I looked up what 'to herald' means and it is someone who carries official messages. Another meaning is a person or thing viewed as a sign that something is about to happen. Jean Shinoda Bolen talks about the third wave of Feminism. First was the Suffragette movement, the second the political women's movement. This third wave has to do with bringing women's wisdom and spirituality into the World.[3]

I was trying to think of a skilful question to end on and it might be something like this. What is the wisdom that the crane is trying to show to us at this time. What do you think the wisdom of the crane is trying to tell you? If like the Crane, we have been holding onto the stones for so long. When will we become more awakened? Will the noise of the stones falling eventually wake us up?

Rockabill Reflection:

Personal: I think the crane has returned now to reveal to me my inner wisdom. I know I deny that I have wisdom to share. Crane is saying no to that – share your wisdom. It may be what someone else needs to hear.

Planetary: Who knows why the crane left Ireland? It may have been weather. I think the return of the crane may be signalling the need to return to a more nature-based way of living so we can tap into the wisdom of the Earth again.

Notes

Introduction

1. Blackie (2016)
2. Cousineau (2001)
3. O'Connor (2000)

Mythology

1. Whelan (2006)
2. Thompson & Schrempp (2020)
3. Paul Rebillot (2006)
4. Williams, David Lewis (2002)
5. Campbell, Joseph & Moyers, Bill (1991)
6. Thompson & Schrempp (2020)
7. Campbell (1991)
8. Terri Wilding (2005)
9. Clarissa Estes Pinkola (1995)
10. Karen Armstrong (2005)
11. Thompson & Schrempp (2020)
12. Ibid
13. O'Hogain (1999)
14. Jason Kirby (2009)
15. Anthony Murphy (2017)
16. Patricia Monaghan (2003)
17. O'Gaoithin, et al (2017)
18. O'Connor (2000)

Wells

1. James MacKillop
2. Celeste Ray
3. ibid

4. Hans Biedermann
5. Rennes Dinchensas
6. Anthony Murphy (2020)
7. Sharon Blackie
8. Martin Brennan
9. Partridge

Rivers

1. Moore (2018)
2. Murphy (2020)

Oceans

1. Rennes Dinchensas
2. Gwynne (1913)
3. Patricia Monaghan
4. Miranda Green
5. Rolf Buamgarten (1986)

Rock

1. Fox (1975)
2. Lobell (1975)
3. Glassman (2011)
4. Newman(2008: 20)
5. O'Crualaoich (1983)
6. Edmund Hogan
7. Judy Hall
8. William and Pearse
9. Thompson
10. Symbolism&methaphor.com
11. New Scientist (2018)
12. Murphy (2017)

Fire

1. Duchas
2. Henry Morris
3. Lenihan (2003)
4. Murphy (2017)
5. O'Hogain (2006)
6. Boris De Kirkoff
7. Lucy Pearce
8. Aniya Sophia
9. Barnhill
10. Ward (2021)
11. O'Connor
12. Krappe

Air

1. Lebor Gabala Eireann
2. O'Curry (P81)
3. Wentz (p292)
4. A. Koltypin (2013)
5. MacRitchie (p369)
6. Wentz (p333)
7. Patricia Monaghan (p262)
8. Carey (p117)
9. Wentz P60
10. Eddie Lenihan
11. S. O'hEochaidh et al (1977)

Afterword

1. Mary Pat Lynch
2. Kallevig (2014)
3. Jean Shinoda Bolen

Bibliography

Balmiers, S (2017) **Who the Hell is Sídhe?** Cailleach's Herbarium.com

Baumgarten, Rolf (1986) **Placenames, Etymology, and the Structure of Fianaigecht** Bealoideas, Folklore Society of Ireland

Benigni, Helen (2013) **The Mythology of Venus: Ancient Calendars and Archaeoastronomy** University Press of America

Bertrand, Azra & Seren (2017) **Womb Awakening: Initiatory Wisdom for the Creatrix of All Life**. Bear and Company

Biederman, Hans (1994) **Dictionary of Symbolism** Penguin Putnam Inc

Blackie, Sharon (2016) **If Women Rose Rooted: Journey to Authenticity and Belonging** September Publishing

Bolen, Jean Shinoda (2001) **Goddesses in Older Women: Archetypes in Women Over Fifty** Harper Collins

Bonwick, James (2011) **Irish Druids and Old Irish Religions** Sovereign Press

Brennan, Martin (1994) **The Stones of Time: Calendars, Sundials, and Stone Chambers of Ancient Ireland** Inner Traditions International

Buttimer, Cornelius G (1981) **Loegaire MacNeill in the Borama** Dept of Celtic Languages and Literature, Harvard University

Campbell, Joseph & Moyers, Bill (1991) **The Power of Myth** Anchor Books

Carey, J (1982) **The Location of the Otherworld in Irish Tradition** Eigse 19 P36-43

Coppens, Philip (2012) Newgrange: **Empowering the Salmon of Wisdom** www.knowth.com

Cousineau, Phil (2001) **Once and Future Myths – The power of ancient stories in our lives** Conari Press

Daimler, Morgan (2016) **Gods and Goddesses of Ireland: A Guide to Irish Deities** Moon Books

Dineen, Rev Patrick S (1927) **Focloir GÁedhilge Agus Bearla** Irish Text Society

Devine, Bit (2014) **On the Path of Druids – Winter Solstice** www.thewildgeese.com

Dooley, Lar (2020) **Out of the Darkness**. The Fairy Council of Ireland

Dorey, Claire (2022) **Drowning in Women's Wisdom: A birth in reverse**. www.magoism.net

Eliade, Mircea (1958) **Patterns In Comparative Religions** Sheed and Ward New York

Elkington, David (2021) **The Ancient Language of Sacred Sound** Inner Traditions

Eogan, G, Kerri Cleay (ed) (2017) **Excavations at Knowth Volume 6: The Passage Tomb Archaeology of the Great Mound at Knowth** Royal Irish Academy Chapter 7 (557,565)

Emerick, Carolyn (2018) **Mythic Dawn** A Journal of European

Mythology ISBN 9781986623711

Fitzpatrick, Kate (2017) **Macha's Twins: A Spiritual Journey with the Celtic Horse Goddess** Immram Publishing

Fox, Michael W (1975) **Animism, Empathy and Human Development** The Humane Society of the United States. Columbia University Press

Glassman, S and Armando, A (2011) **Cities of The Maya in Seven Epochs** McFarlane & Co

Gottlieb, Alma (1986) **Dog: Ally or Traitor** American Ethnologist American Anthropologist Association Vol 13 No3

Graves, Robert (1948) **The White Goddess** A Historical Grammar of Poetic Myth. Farrer, Strauss and Giroux New York

Green, Liz and Juliet Sharman Burke (2000) **The Mythic Journey: The Meaning of Myth as a Guide for Life** Fireside New York

Green, Miranda (1998) **Animals in Celtic Life and Myth** Routhledge New York

Gregory, N (1997) **Comparative Study of Irish and Scottish Logboats** PhD Thesis, University of Edinburgh.

Grigsby, John (2018) **Skyscapes, Landscapes, and the Drama of Proto-Indo European Myth** Doctoral Thesis Bournemouth University

Gwynne, E.J. (1913) **The Metrical Dindsenchas** 5 Vols, Vol 3, Todd Lecture Series 10. Dublin Hodges Figgis

Hall, Judy (2013) **The Crystal Bible 3** Octopus Publishing

Hensey, Robert (2015) **First Light: The Origins of Newgrange** Oxbow Books

Herrstrom, David S (2017) **Light as Experience and Imagination from Paleolithic to Roman Times** Fairleigh Dickinson University Press London

Howard-Gordon, Frances (2016) **Glastonbury Maker of Myths** Gothic Image Publications

Ingold, T (2000:99) **The Perception of the Environment** London Routledge

Irish Jesuit Province EK (1919) **The Boyne and What it Stands For** The Irish Monthly Vol 47 No557

Jones, Carleton (2013) **Temples of Stone: Exploring the Megalithic Monuments of Ireland** The Collins Press

Kattau Colleen (2006) **Women, Water and the Reclamation of the Feminine** Wagadu Volume 3: Spring ISSN: 1545-6196 114 SUNY College at Cortland

Kirby, Jason (2009) **The Salmon In The Spring** Hiraeth Press California

Koberl Nina, (1997) **Quartz: Some of its Uses in Prehistory** Trowel Vol VIII Journal of the Archaeological Society UCD

Koleman, Carol (2007) **Profile of Goddess Bóinn** Catalyst Magazine

Kondratiev, Alexei (2004) **Celtic Rituals: A guide to Ancient Celtic Spirituality** The Collins Press

Koltypin Dr Alexander, **(2013) Website Earthbeforeflood.com**

Krappe, A. H. (1927), **Balor with the Evil Eye**. Studies in Celtic and French Literature, New York, pp. 1–43

Lenihan, E (2003) **Meeting The Other Crowd** Gill Books

Lobell, M (1975) **The Goddess Temple: Humanist Issues in Architecture** Vol 29 No1 Taylor and Francis Ltd

Lundwall, John Knight (2015) **Mythos and Cosmos: Mind and Meaning in the Oral Age** C & L Press Academic Publishing Utah

MacLeod, SP (1998) **Identity and Cross-Correlation in Early Irish Mythology** Dept of Celtic Languages and Literature, Harvard University

MacLeod, SP (2007) **A Confluence of Wisdom: The Symbolism of Wells, Whirlpools, Waterfalls and Rivers in Early Celtic Sources** Dept of Celtic Languages and Literature, Harvard University

MacKillop, James (2005) **Myths and Legends of the Celts** Penguin Books

Mac Ritchie, D (1893) **Notes of the Word Sídhe** Journal of the Royal Society of Antiquaries of Ireland Vol 3 No4 (367-379) Royal Society of Antiquaries of Ireland

Mallory, J.P. (2013) **Origins of the Irish** Thames and Hudson London

Mark, Joshua J (2019) **Dogs In The Ancient World** www.worldhistory.com

Matthews, C & J (1994) **The EncyclopÁedia of Celtic Wisdom** Element Books

Matthews, John (2004) **The Sídhe Wisdom from the Celtic**

Otherworld Lorian Press

Micale, Jenne (2012) **Mothers of Waters: Bóinn and River Goddesses** www.keltria.org

Mitchel, Frank (1992) **Notes on Some Non-Local Cobbles at the Entrances to the Passage – Graves at Newgrange and Knowth**. Journal of the Royal Society of Antiquaries of Ireland Vol122 (128-145) Royal Society of Antiquaries of Ireland

Monaghan, Patricia (2003) **The Red-Haired Girl from the Bog** The Landscape of Celtic Myth and Spirit, New World Library

Moore, Chris et al (2018). **Event and Spirit-Image: Bodily Dismemberment in the East and West and the Logic Surrounding "Consecration"** www.randian-online.com China Art Times Limited (Hong Kong)

Morris, Henry (1927) **Where was Tor Inis, the Island of Fortress of the Formorians?** Journal of the Royal Antiquaries (Vol 17:1)

Morris Henry (1937) **Miscellanea** Bealoideas, Dec 1937 Folklore Society of Ireland P224-227

Murdock, Maureen (1990) **The Heroine's Journey: Woman's Quest for Wholeness** Shambala Publications Inc

Murphy, Anthony (2017) **Mythical Ireland: New Light on the Ancient Past** The Liffey Press

Murphy, A. Moore, R (2020) **Island of the Setting Sun** The Liffey Press

Murphy, Anthony (2021) **Boinn: The Goddess of the River Boyne and the Milky Way** Mythical Ireland Monograph Series No2. Self-Published

Newman, Hugh (2008) **Earth Grids: The Secret Patterns of Gaia's Sacred Sites** Wooden Books Ltd UK

Norman, Ceri (2018) **Faerie Stones: An exploration of the Folklore and Faeries Associated with Stones and Crystals**. John Hunt Publishing

O'Connor, Dr Colm (2015) **The Awakening** Gill and Macmillan

O'Connor, Peter (2000) **Beyond The Mist – What Irish Mythology Can Teach Us About Ourselves** Orion Press

O'Crualaoich, G (2003) **The Book of The Cailleach Cork** University Press

Eugene O'Curry (1855) **Cath Mhuighe Léana, or the Battle of Magh Leana**: The Celtic Society Dublin

O'Donohue, John (2010) **The Four Elements** Transworld Ireland

O'hEochaidh, S et al (1977) **Fairy Legends from Donegal Comhairle** Bhealoideas Eireann

O'Gaoithin, et al (2017) **Lugh Na Bua: The Deliverer** The Onslaught Press

O'hOgain, D (1999) **The Sacred Isle** Collins Press

O'hOgain D, (2006) **The Lore of Ireland: An Encyclopedia of Myth, Legend and Romance**, The Collins Press

Pinkola Estes, Clarrisa (1995) Story As Medicine Michigan Reading Journal

Prendergast, F & Ray T (2002) **Ancient Astronomical Alignments: Fact or Fiction** Archaeology Ireland 16:2 (60

Summer) P35

Prendergast et al (2017) **Facing The Sun**, Archaeology Ireland
Vol31 No4 (17)

Prendergast, Kate (2012) **Archaeology of Mother Earth Sites
and Sanctuaries through the Ages**

Ray, Celeste(2014) **The Origins of Irelands Holy Wells**
Archaeopress Archaeology

Reichard, Joy F (2011) **Celebrate the Divine Feminine:
Reclaiming Your Power with Ancient Goddess Wisdom**
ISBN-13:978-0615904757

Reynolds, F (2009) **Regeneration Substances: Quartz as an
Animistic Agent** The Journal of Archaeology, Consciousness
and Culture (P153-166)

Paul Rebillot (2006) **The Power of Story and Myth** Inside Out,
Vol 48 Journal of IAHAP Ltd

Rionagh Na Ard (2014) **Awakening Life Lessons from the
Sídhe** RavenSídhe Publishing

Roberts, Jack (2016) **The Sacred Mythological Centre of
Ireland** Bandia Publishing

Rochberg, F (2010) **Sheep and Cattle, Cows and Calves: The
Sumero Akkadian Astral Gods as Livestock** Opening The
Tablet Box Brill Publishers

Rua, Áed (2008) **Celtic Flame an Insider's Guide to Irish
Pagan Tradition** Universe Indiana

Shaw, Judith (2016) **Bóinn, Celtic Goddess of Inspiration and
Creativity**

Sherwood, Amy (2009) **An Bó Bheannaithe: Cattle Symbolism in Traditional Irish Folklore, Myth, and Archaeology** PSU McNair Scholars Online Journal Volume 3 Issue

Sjoo, Monica & Barbara Mor (1991) **The Great Cosmic Mother** Harper One

Stout, James Harvey (2018) **The Importance of Myth** Myths-Dreams-Symbols

Taylor, Steve (2018) **Spiritual Science – why science needs spirituality to make sense of the World** Watkins UK

Theuerkauf, Marie Luise (2017) **The Death of Boand and the Recensions of Dindshenchas Erenn**, Eriu, Vol 67 pp 49-97

Thompson, T (2005) **White Quartz in Irish Tradition** Bealoideas Imi 73 P111-133 The Folklore Society of Ireland

Thompson, T, Schrempp, G (2020) **The Truth of Myth** Oxford University Press

Vaughan-Lee, Llewellyn (2017) **The Return of the Feminine and the World Soul** The Golden Sufi Centre

Ward, Karen, B Sexton (2021) **Goddesses Of Ireland** www.moonmna.ie Acrobat Publishing, Dublin

Whelan, Dolores (2006) **Ever Ancient, Ever New: Celtic Spirituality in the 21st Century** Columbia Press

Wilding, Terri (2015) **Stories are Medicine: "healing tales" in myth, folklore, and mythic arts** www.terriwilding.com

Montague Whitsel (2003) **Wellsprings of the Deer: A Contemporary Celtic Spirituality** Authorhouse

Williams, David Lewis (2002) **The Mind in The Cave** Thames and Hudson

Wood, Michael (2005) **In Search of Myths and Heroes.**
London: BBC Books

Yuan, Redjade (2013) **The Mysterious Connection between
Sirius and Human** History Online article posted in Astronomy
and Astrophysics and the Cosmos www.iamzhangyuan.com

Appendix

The information about the stone on Rockabill has a number of sources, so I have included this piece to give a flavour of the research that I did on the white vein quartz at Rockabill.

The Age of the Rocks

The Rocks were formed 400 million years ago and come from Caledonian granite and have a special significance among East Coast Granites. Quartz-vein systems are strongly developed throughout. (Ref: Brindley 1972)

Connection with Newgrange Quartz

Several archaeologists have stated that the source of the quartz at Newgrange was Rockabill, including:

George Mitchell (1992).

Robert Hensey, Professor of Archaeology in UCG in his book *First Light: The Origins of Newgrange.* (2015).

Dr George Stavopolous (Eogan et al).

White quartz seems to have been preferentially selected for use at Newgrange (Reynolds 2009).

White Quartz and the Neolithic People

Its visual impact on the landscape and on the peoples who used it must have been considerable. And in turn, this must have been a deciding factor in its deliberate use. (Nina Korbel 1997)

Quartz may have been experienced as fluid, dynamic, and

prone to transformations – continually being worked at, moved and renewed, as part of an ongoing process both human and non-human (Ingold 2000:99).

In Sligo, in nearly every Stone Age interment, fragments of white, smooth, water worn quartz pebbles were found. It is also thought that the stones contained the spirit of their Gods." (Lebour: 1914).

Electrical Properties of White Vein Quartz

Among the most spectacular are the piezo-electric and pyro-electric effects. The piezo-electric effect arises when pressure is applied to the crystal and it produces an electrical spark (most pocket lighters are now powered this way).

The pyro-electric describes the result of variations in temperature, which cause an electrified state of polarity. As the crystal heats up, it first attracts and then abruptly repels the material around it, due to a build-up of electrical charge on its surface (Burgess: 2000).

Pronunciations

Áed   (Aid)
Áine (Awnya)
Bóinn (Bo in)
Bealach (Balack)
Bealtaine (Be al tenah)
Cailleach (Kaliyak)
Chaointe (queenta)
Cuchulainn (Cu culinn)
Cruachan (Crew a con)
Dabhilla (Daw villa)
Dindshensas (Dinchensis)
Gaelige (Gwale ga)
Glas Gabhlin (Glass Gavlin)
Loughcrew (Lock crew)
Lughnasadh (Lu nasa)
Maebh (Mave)
Neachtain (Knock tin)
Oengus (En gus)
Samhain (Sow win)
Segais (Seggish)
Sídhe (Shee)
Tuatha Dé Danann (Tooha Day Danann)
Uisneach (Ish knock)

Acknowledgements

Team Trish for this book is a large group and I wish I could name everyone.

To Sharon Blackie and Anthony Murphy whose writings inspired me to write this book in the first place.

To Amantha, Anna, Dolores, Enda, Judith, Mel, Michael and Siofra, thank you so much for taking the time to read and comment on the book, it was invaluable to me.

To my various circles of women: Skerries Women's Circle who have encouraged me at every meeting.

To Seana, Miriam, Lorraine and Niamh thank you for the friendship and constant support.

To my Super Women group Clodagh, Liz F and Liz G, Martina, Alison, Triona, Barbara and Sandra for all your cheering and sharing.

My fellow shamanic travellers Emma, Regula, Francesca, Eva, Maria, Blainaid, Vikki and Elaine for all your wise words. To the wonderful Amantha Murphy whose wisdom has helped me beyond words to write this book.

To the sisterhood I have found at the Unbound Press. The mastermind group and the team. Your unconditional presence and feedback have been so valuable to me. Nicola, thank you for listening to your soul's calling. I am so glad I found you. Every word, idea, and suggestion comes from your heart and soul and it is so special – Rock on Unbound!

To The Rock On women Bernie, Ger, Jean and Naomi; thanks, you wonderful wise women.

To my dearest friend Anne Keating, we have known each other for fifty years and you have always been there for me through all the tears and the cheers – thank you.

The DLHF crew for always having my back, thanks.

To my family the Murphy's, the Langton's, too many to list, for always being ready to talk about the book. Shout out to Gerry Murphy and Tony Murphy for helping me with the website.

To Ian, Graham, Claire, Sophie, Simon, Hannah, Remi and Nicole – my heart and soul. You were a beautiful distraction when I needed it most.

To the constant rock in my life Declan Langton, who has stood by me through thick and thin, supported me in every way he could to write this book, much love, and thanks for all of it.

About the Author

Patricia is a mother, grandmother, celebrant, shamanic practitioner, healer, stone whisperer, and bibliophile.

She has an academic background in Psychology and Social Policy. Patricia retired early in her career as a Health Education Officer and now spends time facilitating women's circles and leading rituals in her hometown of Skerries in Dublin Ireland.

Her passions include visiting Neolithic stone monuments, singing and composing sacred chants, writing poetry, and occasionally dancing. She is married to husband Declan and her extensive book collection.

This is Patricia's first book, which for her is a lifelong dream now fulfilled.

Contact Details

You can reach Patricia in the following ways:

Facebook – Ancient Rockabill

Instagram – Patricia.langton.5

Website – irishstonecrone.ie

Ingram Content Group UK Ltd.
Milton Keynes UK
UKHW011817080523
421421UK00005B/376